S0-AVW-590

Turkey Rediscovered

Turkey Rediscovered

by
Klaus Reichert

Translated from the German by
Eugene H. Hayworth

Armchair Traveller
at the bookHaus

First published as *Türkische Tagebücher*
by Klaus Reichert
© S. Fischer Verlag GmbH, Frankfurt am Main, 2011

Published in Great Britain in 2016 by
The Armchair Traveller at the bookHaus Ltd
70 Cadogan Place
London SW1X 9AH

English translation copyright © Eugene H. Hayworth, 2016

This book is sold subject to the conditions that it shall not, by way of trade
or otherwise, be lent, resold, hired out or otherwise circulated without the
publisher's prior consent in any form of binding or cover other than that in
which it is published and without a similar condition including this condition
being imposed on the subsequent purchaser.

A CIP record for this book is available from the British Library

ISBN 978-1-909961-08-1
eISBN 978-1-909961-09-8

Typeset in Garamond by MacGuru Ltd
Printed in Spain by Liberdúplex

www.hauspublishing.com

Contents

Preface

What is it that brings someone to Turkey, except to come as a tourist on a holiday, an archaeologist or a language student? Yet Turkey – apart from Istanbul, a few resorts on the Mediterranean, and a few excavated Middle Eastern, Greek and Roman cities – is still an undiscovered country, despite its immense cultural and scenic riches.

In 2008 Turkey was to be the host country for the Frankfurt Book Fair. In preparation, the Goethe-Institut, as in former and future appearances from guest countries at the fair, had the idea, in cooperation with the literature houses, to send a dozen German-language writers to Turkey to keep an Internet journal 'on-site' and send it to the Goethe-Institut in Istanbul (for translation and dissemination). In return, the same number of Turkish authors would be sent to German cities during the exhibition.

Maria Gazzetti, then the director of the Literature House in Frankfurt am Main, recommended me as an author, because she knew of my desert journal from Sinai and my interest in early cultures. From among the cities that were available I chose Urfa, a provincial capital in southeastern Anatolia near the Syrian border, because Urfa had been the ancient city of Edessa and a point of intersection – or rather, a multi-layering – of the cultures of the ancient Orient since the time of the Sumerians. Later in the year I was able to travel back to Turkey in the same programme, to the Aegean Sea, in an area with very different historical layers.

The trips were coordinated and organised by the Association of Literature Houses, in cooperation with the Goethe-Institut in Istanbul and the Ministry of Culture in Ankara. The Literature House in Munich took the leading role on the German side; the coordinator there was Claudia Nolte.

I cannot praise enough the tireless efforts or the enthusiasm and the implementation strategies of Claudia Hahn-Raabe, the head of the Istanbul Institute, and her team of breathtaking bilingual speakers, including Fügen Ugur.

The writers-in-residence had the best translators at their sides throughout their stay (and, when necessary, a car and driver). This made it possible to learn something about the people through conversation which a tourist unfamiliar with the language does not learn. I was fortunate twice: on the trip to Urfa Şenay Karakoc, an interpreter from Izmir, accompanied me, and Ülker Sayin, a cultural scientist from Istanbul, was with me on the journey on the Aegean Sea.

I had prepared myself for the journey, not through the study of 'leaders', but by reading some works of ancient history, supplemented with books by travellers in the country such as

Xenophon and Moltke, both military men with a strategist's eye for landscape and terrain.

I travelled light: a Turkish dictionary, a grammar book, a novel by Orhan Pamuk (from Anatolia), and a translation of the *Iliad* by Count Stolberg (in the Aegean). No travel guide. I am not sharing what I have read, but I am writing about what I have heard through the medium of my translators. (According to Herodotus, the Greek verb 'historein' means: go, look, listen, explore, and then write about it.) There are two additional essays I wrote for this book on things that particularly fascinate me about Turkey: one about the little-known, major architect Sinan, the master builder for Suleiman the Magnificent in the sixteenth century, and another one about Anatolian kilims.

In the summer and autumn of 2010, the journals were revised, facts corrected, and quotations inserted, especially from Moltke's astonishing letters home, which are hardly known anymore today. (Helmuth von Moltke, *Briefe über Zustände und Begebenheiten in der Türkei aus den Jahren 1835 bis 1839*, 8th edition, edited by G. Hirschfeld, Berlin: Mittler, 1917.)

I offer my thanks to the Goethe-Institut, Claudia Hahn-Raabe and Fügen Ugur in Istanbul, Clemens-Peter Haase in Munich, the Association of Literature Houses and in particular the House of Literature in Munich, as well as Maria Chen Gazzetti in Frankfurt. I am grateful to the Minister of Culture and Tourism in Ankara, Mr Ertogrul Günay, and

Mr. Ibrahim Yazar, who both made it possible for the writers' exchange to take place. My greatest thanks go to the two interpreters, Şenay Karakoc and Ülker Sayin, who never tired of satisfying my curiosity about anything and everything and for their clever questions that got people to open up, even about things they might not have normally revealed to a foreign interviewer. And a very special thank you to Peter Sillem at S. Fischer Verlag, who made this book possible.

K.R., *Frankfurt, January 2011*

Anatolian Journal

Monday, 17 March 2008
On the plane from Frankfurt to Istanbul

Three days ago I bought a pair of running shoes. Camper. The young vendor is a Turk. When he ties my shoe, I see that he does it differently from us: first a loop, then through it he pulls a second one, resulting in a double bow (not a double knot). I ask him why he does not tie the bow 'like we do'. "Oh, there are twenty ways to tie a shoe. I learned this bow from my aunt. She died and I could not go to her funeral. Every time I tie this bow, I think of my aunt – a hundred times a day..." I tell him where I am going to spend the next four weeks. He says: "In Urfa there are *köfte*, the best meatballs in the world."

Turkish Airlines, first row, window seat. The view outside: dense, sunlit clouds, a polar landscape. Sometimes turbulence. Below: green or brown flat rectangles, when the blanket occasionally opens up. But no mountains, no sea, in spite of the already two-hour flight.

Now, nearly three o'clock our time, only a few clouds can be seen. We are over the sea, and there emerges an almost perfectly straight coastline. Sand; furrowed sea; hilly, forested

1

land; and, in between, lakes. Very cramped settlement, a forest of houses. Now something comes into view which has to be the Sea of Marmara. Many ships.

In Istanbul Fügen Ugur, from the Goethe-Institut, picks me up. She speaks flawless German. A two-hour delay, during which she tells me about Urfa. There is a very active group of young women who are committed to the rights of women directed against men – fathers, brothers, uncles, cousins – against the 'code of honour'. Urfa is the centre of huge dams that have caused many problems. Kurdish villages were resettled, their areas flooded. The recent irrigation resulted in salinisation of the soil, and therefore barrenness.

One-and-a-half hour flight to Urfa. Arrival in the evening. Şenay Karakoc, the interpreter who is to accompany me for the four weeks, also arrived. Long journey by car through pistachio plantations which are not visible in the dark. The Hotel El Ruha – the Arabic name for Urfa, City of the Winds – a new five-star castle, in the style of the old, demolished houses of the city that are built with the local, white-yellow stone, *Urfa taş*, Urfa stone. There is no alcohol in the hotel, located across from the grotto of Abraham's birth – the Prophet Ibrahim – because it is a holy place, apparently surrounded by concentric suburbs. The view from my window looks across to a huge, elongated citadel, crouching on a high cliff like a primordial animal. About ten o'clock, after the late dinner (*kofte*!), we walk in the direction of the rock through a park, to the famous pond where carp swarm in the light of the nearly full moon:

holy carp. Steps down and up, old walls, a Koran school for girls. Everything spotlessly clean, will be swept again even at midnight; flagstone paths are awash, so that you can easily slip and fall. Somehow spic and span – unlike how I imagine an Anatolian province city – but perhaps all fake. Between two minaret towers a green neon sign vacillates, blinking on and off, 'City of the Prophet'. I want to know who but Ibrahim is still counted here.

In one single hotel there should be wine. The waiter makes a dubious face, says yes, but the refrigerator was broken. That did not matter, and his face is even more dubious. Half an hour later he comes back and places a bottle in front of us. Could he not open it? He has no corkscrew; neither do we. After another half an hour he has found one and leaves us to open the bottle ourselves. Is the influence of the prophets so drastic that even touching the wine – the potential contact, the smell – would contaminate the faithful? Probably the completely mistaken night thoughts of a traveller who has prepared himself to find every gesture strange, and therefore meaningful. The waiter is probably just tired or lazy.

Tuesday, 18 March 2008
With Fügen and Şenay, down the hill to the park that looked so much like a mediocre Disneyland last night. Certainly, the stones of the walls blaze yellow-white and look like new in the hot sun, but almost everything is old, just unexpectedly well maintained. A mecca. Two mosques dating from the twelfth

century; another, even older, from the eighth; one from the seventeenth. Here once stood the cathedral with the bones of doubting Thomas, which were transferred in the third century from South India to Edessa, as Alexander named the city.

I remember that Thomas was called the twin of Jesus, and that he, because he was the only one who had physical contact with the risen Jesus, was the recipient of the secret words of Revelation. Şenay says that the sick King Abgar of Edessa had written a letter to Jesus, who had sent an answer because he believed in him, without seeing him, that he would heal him. "Your city will be blessed, and henceforth the curse will no longer prevail over it." Jesus also sent his image, and it should still be here somewhere, "the oldest icon of Christ," Şenay says. Afterwards, Thomas later sent an apostle, Thaddeus (or was he himself the one who journeyed forth?), and founded the church in Edessa. On what ground here do we stand?

To enter the grotto of Abraham's birth I have to remove my shoes and socks, and duck through a narrow wall opening, crawling more than slipping through. In the hazy, small room, separated from the grotto by a glass wall, men kneel in a position of prayer. The grotto is full of water which, it seems, gushes into the room through a concrete basin. The men drink the holy water from metal cups and nod their heads rhythmically. As I am leaving I see a servant with a large thermos bottle, who replenishes the water in the basin. It is noticeable to the newcomer that the sacred, the miraculous, and the utterly profane not only do not disturb, but are quite normal.

Back outside, the Müezzin sings the noon prayer with the climax of the sun. A lot of men, but also women, hurry into the mosques, swiftly throwing away cigarettes. At the same moment the paths paved with Urfa stone are full of people who simply walk, ignoring the Müezzin and feeding the fat carp: thousands of carp that cannot be eaten because they are holy. For all their holiness they are scrambling around a bit in an earthly way for the food that, in portions sold in aluminum tins, is snatched greedily, especially by the fattest ones. I would like to know if they dispose of themselves, the carp, when their hour has struck. But what else can they do? Where can they go?

Next, on to the market which is considered the finest in Turkey. Everything is well ordered: meat with meat, vegetables with vegetables, fabric with fabric, coppersmiths with the coppersmiths. Not a single souvenir or gift shop. No merchant is trying to draw anyone into his shop; the stranger is not even approached. The dealers are proud of their merchandise; they explain the difference between freshly roasted pistachios and those from last Autumn and we can taste the difference. The best paprika (biber) is made when the pods are dried in the sun for a long time and then mixed with oil. Prices are in lira, not in dollars or euros. Everything is busy and quiet – but slow and thoughtful at the same time, as in the days determined by the everyday needs of people, both those living here in the city or in the surrounding villages.

Suddenly the alley of the covered market empties out into a sweeping, square, two-story courtyard. Routine Renaissance architecture, not at all 'oriental' – no battlements, no steeple, no domes – built by Suleiman the Magnificent in the sixteenth century. Old, very tall, weathered Sycamore trees, many tables where men sit across from other men and play chess. Or Tavla: Backgammon.

Şenay explains: 30 pieces for the number of days in the month, 4 times 6 wedges for the 24 hours, 12 white and 12 black wedges for day and night, 4 zones for the seasons. This is the basic measurement of time that is given us. But we Westerners must blindly roll the dice in order to play our game of life, and the system gets muddled by laws that only the goddess of fortune knows.

A man with a tea tray walks through the rows and shouts "Chai". Many children with shoe cleaning kits. Another man runs around with a scale and shrilly offers his services. A big, heavy man lets himself be weighed and the weigher takes the weight of all the parts of his body, which carries too many pounds. Content, the fat man dismounts: his corpulence is complacently comfortable. No one can say to him, "Weighed and found wanting."

We rush back to the hotel, because we have an appointment with a young lady who cares about the rights of women. Hanan is 29 and has brought her 11-year-old daughter, a lovely child who listens attentively. 'Violence against women' is the focus of the organisation that Hanan heads. She attended the eight-year primary school, is a trained felt maker (for all intents and purposes a man's job, which requires a great deal of strength), and is at the same time currently completing her high school diploma and then wants to study art. She says that over the past five years a lot has changed in the province – girls are now allowed to attend schools and study without opposition from their fathers, uncles, brothers or cousins; husbands have permitted their wives to work. Perhaps that had something to do with the work of women's organisations? Certainly. But there is still so much to do. There are still the well-known forced marriages, but much less, and affairs of honour. (She does not talk about honour killings. I will have to ask her about that the next time.) Have there been problems with the Kurds due to the resettlements, or is it that just a few kilometres further east in northern Iraq, the Turkish Air Force is fighting the PKK? "No, absolutely not. Urfa had a Kurdish population of more than 40 per cent. They lived together with the Turks and Arabs, often in the same houses, in a completely ordinary neighborhood. We respect each other's differences across so many similarities."

At half past three we head off to visit the governor of the province of Urfa, who has offered to receive us. In the end it was the Turkish Ministry of Culture which paid for the German authors' travel and accommodations. Mr. Yavaşcan is an elegant, gracious gentleman 'in the prime of life' and he is excited about the treasures of his city and his province – near here is the Garden of Eden where the pomegranate trees still stand; not far off was Noah's Mount Ararat, and the gazelles which had suckled Abraham – (surely we would have already visited the grotto of his birth?) – still grazed in the area; Isaac and Rebecca had married here; the oldest of all mankind's sculptures had been unearthed here; the 'Urfa Man', which we must absolutely view tomorrow at the Archaeological Museum, is here again after it was lent to Karlsruhe last year. He proudly displays the poster. He takes time for us, wants to understand one thing or another, drinks tea with us, gives us gifts (baskets and mats, catalogs, a CD about Urfa) and has only one complaint: There is no tourism. I do not say: "Allah'a Şükür! Be glad, because then your proud Urfa would be lost. Don't even let it become an insider's tip, because we know the fate of insider's tips." I do not say anything. He is a politician, and I do not know the economic condition of the city and the province except that of the dam, which presents insurmountable problems. With an "Insh' Allah" we diplomatically take our leave.

Wednesday, 19 March 2008

After breakfast we want to go up to the fortress and we choose the underground tunnel, a winding staircase with very high, steep steps cut into the rock. By the hundredth step I must calm my pounding heart. Above, a wide view on three sides overlooking the never-ending city on the horizon. The vast fortress plateau has few remnants of ruins, just two columns on the rampart facing the city, seventeen metres high, with Corinthian capitals. The columns are said to have been the catapult from which Abraham, that pious man of God, was hurled down into the fire, which then turned into the water with the carp. This was the time of King Nimrod – 'He was a mighty hunter before the Lord' (or should that read 'Against the Lord'?) – in the third millennium. The columns date back to the fourth century BCE and bear the inscription of an Aramaic king who described himself as a son of the sun. I cannot remember who built everything up here, destroyed, expanded, rebuilt, and destroyed it again – Stone Age people, the Sabians, the Hittites, the Assyrians, Alexander, the Sassanids, the Syrians, the Greeks, the Romans. From Roman times, the area was part of the northernmost province of Mesopotamia. One of the cruelest emperors, Caracalla, was murdered here. During, or after, the Second Crusade Baldwin of Bouillon, the brother of Godfrey, fortified the castle and established a county here that existed for more than one hundred years. Then the Mongols came, led by Timur the Lame, and destroyed everything.

On the side facing town a fortified moat several metres deep safeguarded the stronghold against attacks from the east. (Therefore the Mongols could only take it by treachery, as previously the Romans had taken the Volscian and Ernici castles that were fortified by colossal walls.) On the other side of the moat a settlement was created from the stones of the fort. The garbage is disposed of over the wall of the settlement – stoves, refrigerators, televisions, car tires, the usual plastic waste – I see it for the first time in the otherwise neat city, accumulating there among the fig trees.

Descent into the valley over wide stone steps. Cypresses, pines, palm trees, plane trees, eucalyptus, pines, even osier. A small, brownish pigeon flies in circles around a flock. The pigeons are sacred to the prophets; when the prophets were on the run the pigeons built a nest for them in a cave.

To the market with Şenay in the late afternoon. Along the carpet and kilim road all the stores but one are already closed because today is a holiday; home in the evening, when every believer prays for forgiveness of his sins. Children carry baked goods to the neighbours. The shops all look the same: a single small cavernous room. The merchant sits in his Aladdin's Cave between and in front of pillars of folded, uniformly-stacked kilims that glow in all the colours of the Orient. He displays kilim after kilim like illuminated manuscripts in front of us, and has yet an even more lavish one to display, names the places of origin (according to colours, patterns), the age, exciting himself and us with the colours, the irregular patterns. Foreigners do not come to him; they do not exist. He has taken over the business, where he has worked since he was 8 years old, from his father. One son has a large carpet business out by the roadside, the other studies philosophy and sociology in Istanbul. Şenay says: "We are his Kismet – all the other shops are closed because of the holiday."

About ten o'clock, at the top of the hotel terrace. The near-full moon is high in the east, at an estimated angle of 60 degrees to the earth. It is white and starkly bright, with a very wide corona in bright spectral colours: a painting by Turner. A single star still above – which one? Scattered stars all around, but no recognisable constellations because of the exceptional brightness below and above. An icy southeasterly wind blew all day.

Journal writing. Now, about one o'clock, the moon has moved towards the south. Its corona has dissolved; jagged clouds surround it. The city, noisy during the day and into the evening, is silent. In the distance a barking dog, a raven, the wail of another bird; I think I can even hear the jumping carp in the waters of Abraham. Then, a street sweeper with his rattling metal trolley.

Thursday, 20 March 2008

Driving southeast by car in the direction of Syria to the old city of Harran. In the west, elongated mountain ranges; in the east, open country with cornfields that are already green – the once barren land is crisscrossed with concrete trenches which receive their water from the dam. Around Harran the region is barren, stony, chalky, wasteland, desert. From the city, that existed a long time before the Assyrians, and was eventually conquered by them, there are preserved remains: city walls; one of the four gates; the remains of the mosque that was previously a church, and which before that was the temple of the moon god Sin, the two-gendered god, who was worshiped under a full moon as a female and under the new moon as a male deity. (Harran was the centre of the Moon cult; Sin is the highest of the Assyrian gods. The reigns of dynasties were each under the patronage of one of the planets – when Venus 'reigned', Nineveh was the capital – but at the end of time the moon would complete the cycle and reign for all eternity. But before the Assyrians, Sin was the god of the Sabians and originally the god of the Nomads, who covered their caravans at night. Cults layer after layer on top of each other.)

Abraham and Laban were here until the brothers parted because there was not enough room for the herds. Abraham moved on. Alexander one or two thousand years later, the Seleucids, the Arnmäer, the Romans, the Caliph. Where has all the glamour gone? Perhaps, except in our minds, it is still lying under the debris left behind by the Mongols, which no one has removed in the past eight hundred years and which we now walk over on goat paths? There is still a tower, an observatory, which allegedly belongs to the University, the oldest of Islam, which was founded by the Sassanids. Here Battani calculated the distance of the moon from the earth; here Jabir ibn Hayyan suggested the idea of atomic fission: a single part of an atom could destroy a city like Baghdad; here the doctor Zekeriya Razi said he believed in God but not in the Prophet, and he was allowed to say that. All these things happened in the ninth century, while we were still struggling in the West, learning to read and write. Debris, meager grassland, a few lost sheep and goats.

Two women in colourful loose robes are sitting on the ground: a heavyset old one with a round moon face, and a slender one, no longer young. We greet them and they invite us to join them for tea. They send the inquisitive boy who has been accompanying us the entire time to the mud huts, which are not far from here. We ask about the piles of brush that are stacked everywhere – cylindrical structures that narrow from the bottom up, similar to the Trulli houses next door. (Why have the people here devised forms that are equal to each other in diameter and height and yet – in what way? – are distinct, recognisable in their own right, precious stuff that must last over the winter? Distinguishable thanks to their location? In relationship to the huts? To the points of the compass? But where does the 'will to form' *this* form come from? The pile as a serial form? Giving order to anything that is arbitrarily lying around, like Richard Long.) These were cotton-wool brush piles separated by families, the only combustible material, because they had no cow or camel dung to light.

The women speak only Turkish that is difficult to understand. They are Arabs: "All of us here are Arabs!" I ask (I know that there are Syrian Christians in the area) whether they are Muslims. As if she was shooing away a fly, the old one wipes away the question as stupid or incomprehensible with a flick of her hand and says: "We are all children of the Prophet." I ask how many children she has, and she indicates with her fingers: 6 sons and 2 daughters. (Now as I recall her heavy body, squatting as if giving birth, she seems to me like a Sumerian earth or mother or fertility goddess.) But, she continues with the same wave of the hand as before. They have all up and left. None of the children come to visit her. So what does she live for? She works in the cotton fields. The money she earns there in

13

summer must last till the next summer. In the meantime, the daughter of the frail woman, who has ten children, has come with the tea. Those who put sugar into the glass murmur at the same time: "Bless God!" A third elderly woman passes by on the way to the next village, drops a heavy sack and sits down. She explains something in nimble Arabic. The three women laugh and comment. The young woman, the daughter, is silent and looks sadly into the distance. As we take our leave, Şenay puts a few coins on the tea tray. They are thrown back at his feet almost magisterially. The old woman says: "If someone comes into my garden and takes something, he is supposed to pay for it. If I give him something, it is a gift!"

In front of the ramparts of Harran are the so-called Trulli houses, round brick houses with conical pointed roofs: beehives. They are spacious and seem to be even more spacious, because you can go from house to house from inside. These houses are recent – only two or three hundred years old. The Trulli square surrounds an open courtyard, where you can entertain strangers and friends. In the courtyard there is a wooden device to which a goat hide is suspended by its four legs. Its mouth is open. Milk and water are poured into it, and the device is shaken until the ayran is blended. Why such an ingenious device, where otherwise everything is so simple? Perhaps because there is still something of the spirit of the goat alive in the hide and conveys itself in the potion?

On the street in front of Harran there are a few shops where Şenay wants to buy fruit and water. I remain in the car and observe the people who are standing there or stride by with measured steps. Suddenly I feel that I know many of the faces from the museums: Sumerians, Hittites, Assyrians, Syrians, Greeks, Romans, the conquerors and conquered, the masters and slaves...

The journey continues through rocky desert land to the large caravanserai, the Han Ed Barur, (which is what goat dung is called), at the intersection of the east–west and north–south trade routes. There must have been room for dozens of caravans and hundreds of camels in this magnificent compound, which is still almost intact. The owner of the Han became rich in the raisin trade. It is said he predicted that nothing of this place would remain but goat manure. He must have been a far-sighted man – the soil, covered everywhere by small shillelaghs of sheep dung, resembles emptied sacks of raisins.

We continue on the asphalt road. Sometimes the road is smooth, sometimes bumpy because of water damage. The settlements that occasionally appear along the road or deeper in the desert consist of a few neatly built, humble mud huts. Walls and flat roofs: dark brown, evenly-grouted clay. Under the clay on the roofs is a layer of timber or brushwood. The window holes, if they exist, are so narrow you cannot poke your head through them. Sometimes colourful laundry flutters in the wind. Individual goats and sheep.

To the town – four, five houses – of the Prophet Şuayb, who is accepted here as the father-in-law of Moses and corresponds to the Jethro of the Bible. While we search for the well that he 'resurrected' and the cave where he lived, a flock of happy children surrounds us, jumping like goats at breakneck speed into underground passageways and popping up again somewhere behind or in front of us; children, showing their feats, not calling "hello, money, money", as you sometimes hear in the streets of Urfa. It occurs to me what diverse skin tones the children have, from bright white to more brownish, almost black. Since it cannot be assumed that the fathers and forefathers have moved away from the region or emigrated into it, one can draw the conclusion that the many ethnic groups who passed through here have – over the long term of Mendelian laws – left their mark.

In Şuayb's cave you can find engravings from the Stone Age which the prophet must have encountered: stick figures, animals with horns (Ibex? Gazelles?) Next to the grotto a prayer room with kilims has been laid open to the public. In front there is a bare, so-called 'wishing tree', draped with many colourful slips of paper. There is no such tree in Islam, says Şenay. It must go back to older, shamanistic customs imported from Central Asia. We continue on to Sumatar, the 'Regensdorf', to the cultic site of the Sabeans, which must have existed long before 2000 BCE, long before Moses. In a circle around a natural depression in the nearby or further distance, there are seven mountains which were consecrated to the seven planets. We climb the nearest mountain, the one of the Sun, and from there we can spot the other mountains. It's simply breathtaking to realise, that not only prior to the start of history an entire, vast landscape had been designated as a sanctuary, a sacred ground, but also what knowledge of the heavenly bodies the Sabeans possessed. The mountain consecrated to Saturn is the furthest. You would like to take off your shoes, as God asked of Moses at the burning bush. There it was just a spot in front of a bush; here it is an expanse, wherever you look. As far as I can see with binoculars, sanctuaries on the mountains – built or hewn – no longer exist. At the top of the Sonnenberg is a relief of the sun god (with corona), carved into the rock; next to it, at a distance, the bas-relief of a female figure. Both are certainly from a later period. We decide to return and to wander the planets from mountain to mountain.

We climb down over meagre grass full of dandelions, angel's eyes, and carline thistles from the previous year. A big herd of sheep come to meet us – certainly more than a hundred animals – with a few lambs and goats, long-haired, shaggy fellows who are waiting to be sheared when winter is over. A young man on a donkey shoos them uphill and they follow, crowded together. A big dog looks out sedately from a rock and lets the horseman take care of his duties. The dog has a sandy, short, sleek coat and a skull in which the three-headed hellhound has become one. I would not want to encounter him alone. The breed is called Sivas-Kangal and is only found here in the region. Eventually the flock is scattered all over the hillside, pure white, slowly wandering dots like fleecy clouds in the sky. At some point they are herded together again, and descended like braids down the slope, like the hair of the beloved in the *Song of Songs*, which descended like a flock of sheep down from Mount Gilead.

People here also have stories to tell about Moses and his father-in-law. Here Şuayb gave Moses the rod with which he struck the water from the rock. The guard leads us to the place: a deep well. "Here," – he points to grooves in the shaft wall – "you can still see how Moses [Musa] jolted the rock." It was, the guard tells us, the same rod which Şuayb sent with Moses to the Pharaoh, to move him through his magic tricks to release the children of Israel. Şuayb also gave Moses one of his daughters in marriage. Moses did not want that one, but rather the other, "because he had seen her foot while she was drawing water." In view of so much living traditional lore I grow uncertain: Does the story now 'take place' up here in Anatolia, in the northernmost Mesopotamia, or down in the land of Midian in Egypt? Did the writer of Exodus bring it down and adapt its tradition or did the Mohammedans bring it up? (But yes, I know: Mohammed, who adapted so many biblical stories for the Koran, did not cite them. He reflects how he has heard them on his desert walks around the campfires, told by Bedouins like our guard.) But what does it matter? Stories are just stories, derived from other stories, leading to other stories, genuine originals, genuine imitations, variations of an original that does not exist. It comes down to telling good stories, and the guard does not want to finish; he regards it as overtime. Şenay does not even translate, but he

18

repeats at the same time and accompanies his speech with a whole sign language dictionary, because I do not understand his words.

We still need to see the cave – human figures in bas-relief, larger than life: a head with horns, the cult figure of Marilaha, the God of all gods (pre-Mosaic). Above and next to the statues there are old Aramaic inscriptions (post-Mosaic). Above the cult figure someone has inscribed a cross.

Suddenly we are on the go, cries of children from innumerable throats. Between planet cults, biblical sheep, Moses, Şuayb and a horned God, we had not noticed that there is a school in the narrow valley. It is recess and the girls and boys frolic in the playground – the girls in blue school uniforms, the boys in suits with bow ties, the pretty teacher in a colourful short dress and a headscarf. What do they care about Moses and his father? They are children, like children everywhere, and the teachers come from the big cities and are 'conscripted' here for two years. There are two bus drivers standing by; they are waiting until school is out, about five o'clock. Now it's just after four. Then they take the children back to their families in the scattered mud huts.

While walking to the car we pass a bare tree, where a large swarm of brown birds above are outdoing each other in excited chirping – nightingales, greenbuls. On the way back a flock of sheep cross the road. We stop. A huge Sivas-Kangal barks at us and runs alongside the moving car, wanting to encircle it. If he could, he would devour us. Maybe he has in him the power

19

and dynamics of an ancient God who demands his human sacrifice for the desecration of holy soil.

Friday, 21 March 2008

All morning fighting the computer again and trying to send pictures. How I hate these things, because they steal my energy and life. Without Şenay I would be lost.

Then to the small but very fine Archaeological Museum. Here stands the famous Stone Age man, who for the time being is the oldest representation of humanity, from about 9000 BCE. A massive, slightly larger-than-life half-figure made of limestone, the surface gently smoothed, barely polished. Somewhat uncivilised – it could also be the body of a demon or an idol – but with a clear sense of human proportions. The head is a little too big, egg-shaped with a thick nose and close-fitting ears plugged with blue sparkling obsidian which I thought at first were eye sockets. Stone Age man must therefore have known the value of this rare stone. Where had it come from? In the area of Urfa, where the man was excavated (more precisely: right next to my hotel during the excavation work), the stone did not exist. Through trade? Bartering? But with whom? And where? The arms, somewhat awkwardly angled from the shoulders, cross hands over his genitals; to the left and right the testicles are clearly carved out. A fertility symbol, centuries before female figures took on this role?

A slender boar with frightening tusks, a bull of brownish limestone, everything Stone Age. Eye idols – eyes on stalks.

The full moon and the beginning of spring coincide for once, which is why our Easter is so early. Across the country, the beginning of spring is celebrated with music. However, there is a fear of political demonstrations. The police are on alert.

Saturday, 22 March 2008

In a northeasterly direction to the settlement established by Adam and Eve after their expulsion from paradise, as the Governor knows – Göbekli Tepe, 'Potbelly Hill', cultivated land – wheat fields, oil – and pistachio trees that already have small conical, reddish flowers. At regular intervals in some fields, it appears to me, there are tidy dried roots which have been pulled-up. There are ancient vines, barely a foot high, which are already putting out shoots, three or four on each cane. The dark brown, sometimes reddish soil is very rocky; where the plow has churned it up, it is loose and soft.

The settlement is located at the top of the slope, with a wide panoramic view of the hill country. That it is supposed to be Adam and Eve's settlement is regrettably an invention, but it is probably the oldest temple of humankind, 9500 BCE, even older than yesterday's Stone Age man. Between small, excavated walls that represent rooms, in an open space on the hillside slope, stand wide, round, flat erected limestone columns, which are completed at the top by equally flat and wide crossbars that extend beyond the edges of the columns: the so-called 'T' column caps. Animal figures have been carved from the stone with incredible realism and precise craftsmanship: roaring lions springing into the air; a bull; a boar with tusks; a crab (how could they know about them?); something that looks like a flattened iguana seen from above – a veritable Noah's ark. The only exception to the realism is an abstract fox in elegant motion – back and tail form a single curve – as if by Brancusi. The guard says that a prehistorian from Heidelberg, Klaus Schmidt, digs here.

Above the site, at the top of the hill, there is a walled circle. In the middle stands a centuries-old mulberry tree hung with wish lists. Could it be that 'göbek' does not mean belly, but navel (which is also a meaning of the word), the convex omphalos as the centre of the earth and the seat of the oracle like the one at Delphi? The lists – today's form of request to the Pythia.

Down the slope again, in front of the archaeological site, maybe two dozen relatively small, cone-shaped holes carved into the polished limestone earth. Everyone who made an offering would have been allocated such a hole for themselves. (How do we know that?) Strange – for more than one offering of grain – did Stone Age man have grain? – one of these holes would hardly be sufficient. And: would everyone have had their own place for sacrifice? Highly unlikely.

Stones, thistles, thorns – that corresponds to the land after the expulsion of Adam, and if God shaped him from this dark plowed earth (adama), then Adam must have been a Moor.

Urfa is full of police and military personnel. Truncheons, shields, fire extinguishers, two armoured tanks near the cemetery. Today the festival for the beginning of spring is celebrated, because yesterday, Friday, the actual holiday, was the Muslim Sunday. On this day – like every year – demonstrations are said to be expected all over the country (PKK, the Left), and the state wants, by way of precaution, to demonstrate its resources and tools. An 83-year-old writer and columnist, Ilhan Selcuk, was said to have been picked up for questioning this morning at four o'clock. When I go to the festival ground in the late afternoon it is empty, and the soldiers withdrawn. An old man murmurs "Salam" and lifts a hand in greeting. I reply to the greeting and raise my hand. When I sense his venomous look, I realise that it was my left hand. Oh God – the foreigner, dealing out misfortune.

Sunday, 23 March 2008
(Easter, according to the Gregorian calendar)

Two-hour drive through a fertile plain, early in the morning, about six o'clock. Irrigation systems sprinkle the wheat fields, chickpeas and lentils. After Mardin we climb high into the barren foothills of the Taurus Mountains. In the hills sometimes, inscribed with stones in huge letters visible from far away, we see: 'I'm proud to be a Turk.' Atatürk.

We want to go to Kirklar Kilisesi, the 'Church of the Forty Martyrs', named after two brothers and their companions, who were killed by their father because they had embraced Christianity. In 569, after he subsequently converted to Christianity, he founded the church, which has been in service since that time and has survived all of the chaos and religious struggle apparently unharmed. The rite is Syriac-Aramaic, the oldest Christian rite ever, as the priest later tells us. It is recorded in large codices in the ancient Syrian language and calligraphy, without neumes or even notes, as I later see. But the faithful know how scripture is to be sung. (Yes, the notes must only be 'written down' for the first time once the communication of traditions has broken down; that is not the case here yet, anyway.)

Gradually the church fills. Men, women, and children crowd in together. Outside it is warm, inside cold, so two roaring potbellied stoves are installed, their big black pipes cutting diagonally across the room. Again and again people move from their benches to one of the stoves and warm their hands. Slowly the service gets under way without a distinct Incipit. Two men have donned white robes; they step up to the table in front of the presbytery which is hidden behind a vestibule and begin to sing from the codices, sometimes alternating with a women's chorus. At some point the curtain, embroidered with a kitschy Last Supper that includes male and female disciples, is raised, and you can see the priest in a splendid robe, who turns away from the congregation, and now, with a high, strained voice, he sings the strange melodies, compared to which our Gregorian chants sounds melodic-harmonious. Of course, I do not understand a word, nor do I understand the rite, which is not reminiscent of any part of the Roman or the Greek. Everything comes from a different time and world long past, but it is not the past here, where it has remained alive and shows in the friendly, cheerful, sharp-nosed faces. Once the priest steps forward with a chalice and a bowl of bread and sings, he puts them both back on the altar again and extends his closed palms to the men serving at the altar, who embrace them with their own hands. The men make the gesture again to their neighbouring believers, who continue it on to the rear bench, on and on until everyone in the room has physically partaken in the blessing. A large bowl of bread – not the one deposited on the altar by the priest – is placed in the front of the church, and the faithful file past and take a piece of ordinary Emek, which is eaten on a daily basis. We will also be asked to take a piece of bread. So there is nothing here of conversion and mystery and the exclusion of other faiths. That is how it goes.

After the two-hour service the priest, Father Gabriel, invites us up into the medieval assembly hall. Bright light streams through the large fluted stone window and the men of the community sit on the walls, smoke and drink a few drops of very strong coffee from small cups. There were seventy Syrian Aramaic families here, says Father Gabriel, about three hundred believers. In the villages around there are just as many who lived peacefully here alongside their Muslim neighbours. Now, at least. In the past there had been problems. (He speaks cautiously.) The everyday language is Aramaic (the language of Jesus), sometimes Arabic, rarely Turkish. But the sacred language Syriac was originally the dialect of Edessa and it became and remained through the translation of the Bible the language of all Syrian Christians. "As Latin is for you," he says in a slightly patronising tone. Incidentally, the Syrian script – I had seen it in the folios – evolved from the old Kufic script of the Arabic in which the Koran is written. So the teachers of the Arabs up until the eighth or ninth century were also the teachers of Islam.

Why then don't they celebrate Easter today, I want to know, but four weeks later? They only had the Julian calendar, the only accurate one, and he goes into a long explanation about why it had been wrong – "A distortion of the faith, outrageous, to eliminate eleven of the days individually numbered by God!" – of Pope Gregory in 1582 to shift the calendar that was named after him.

When the men leave, one by one, they touch their fingertips to those of the priest, and then direct them to their lips and bow. We vigorously shake his hand.

From the high-altitude of Mardin we should have a view far down over the Tigris and the Mesopotamian plain. But today the sky has swallowed up the sun. There is only a hazy curtain, which does not rise. Perhaps the long-awaited view would have been disappointing – like a gift that is not appropriate.

We continue up into the mountains to the Deyrulzafaran Monastery, from the fifth century, which is named after the saffron-coloured stone. Once, there was a sun temple. They still exhibit the room, built from square stone blocks weighing several tonnes. It contains the sacrificial altar and the porthole through which the rising sun shone. The monastery – a large courtyard, corridors with cells for the monks – was once the seat of the Patriarch of the Syrian Christians. Inside the church are the heavy catafalques where the seated patriarchs, facing east, were buried. A Metropolitan bishop and two monks still live here now. It is not a place of silence. There is hammering, sawing and welding; cables and pipes are laid on the Sabbath. The cells are being converted into rooms with showers and heating. You can rent a room here and be a monk for the holiday.

On the return journey, in the plain of Harran, which is also called the 'fertile plain', we make a detour to see the grave of the Prophet Job (Eyyüb). It had been 'known' for a long time that through God's trials and the temptations of Satan (Şeytan) he grew rich again and died here, but it wasn't until the seventeenth century that Sultan Murad IV saw in a dream exactly where the grave was located. There lay the coffin of a giant, under a green blanket, with an equally impressive turban at the head end, in a room with doors of imitation wood. On the sprawling grounds, landscaped with roses for the tourists, you will find the grave of the prophet referred to as Elyasa, Elyesa, and Elisha, one of the friends of Job; then the 'patience stone', where the sorely-tried prophet learned to meditate; and finally, a sacred spring. In the water around it innumerable discordant frogs croak. They are probably taunting me and to be on the safe side I move on quickly. In a grove a little further away is the grave of Job's wife Rahime ('Rahim' means 'uterus').

Oh, how beautiful it was, in the land of Uz, when we could imagine what we wanted.

Monday, 24 March 2008

At the kilim dealer. (Now I write "kilim" like the Turks.) He sits cross-legged on a pile of kilim. We sit on stools, a little lower, in front of him. First he lets Çay come in, then he wants to talk. There will be time for business. His mother was a Kurd, his father an Afghan Turk (or vice versa). They had ten children. "Today, everything is different. I only have three children. And my daughter only has three children. There won't be any more." Do the various nationalities have problems coexisting? "No, we all live together – Turks, Kurds, Arabs, Armenians, everyone respects each other and lets them live as they want." And the PKK? "They do not belong to our group. They live in the mountains, in caves or tents. They dress like the Taliban and all they do is shoot and rob. Sometimes they come to the villages and kill the teachers, because they are teaching the children in Turkish. Many young teachers no longer want to be sent to these areas and would rather change their profession. Anyone who wants to leave the PKK in order to lead a normal life is shot. Now that the military have attacked them in northern Iraq, they have shot their own wounded, so they would not be aided by us and allowed to talk." No, actually he is not interested in politics, he only reads the 'Milliyet' every day and complains that what is going on in the world could make a person sick. "Why don't people leave each other alone?

There is a different way of doing things. We are all human, after all." He does not say: "We are all children of the prophets."

Because it is now time for business, he once again spreads out the treasures from our visit a few days ago. We quickly reach an agreement. He offers us good prices and on those even more of a discount. He will pack them and ship them to Germany tomorrow. Then I pay him for the rest.

I ask him if he also has the black-brown goat hair rugs made by the Bedouins? No, but he knew a merchant – "An honest man!" – who had some. We walk down a few streets through the bazaar and meet the old man, who leads the way and unlocks his shop: roll upon roll of the goat hair canvas in plastic bags, increasingly rarely made today. He slits one open and I see and feel the scratchy, wonderfully energetic work of the nomads. ('The black tents of Kedar', as they are called in the 'Song of Songs'.)

"How long is the roll?"

"27 metres."

"That's too long for me. I was thinking 3 or 4 metres."

"But for a tent, even a little one, you need at least 27 metres …"

"But I don't want to build a tent."

"Oh, you do not want a tent…?"

He thinks that I'm daft. What do you want to do with the stuff? I ask what one metre costs. "Two lira", – one euro. (I once paid Bedouins in the Sinai Desert one hundred euro for one metre, and I was told that I had made a good deal.)

"Good. I'll take the entire roll."

"Allah'a emanet ol!"

Tomorrow the roll, along with the kilims, will travel together to Germany.

Tuesday, 25 March 2008

Muslum Sarac, the kilim dealer, now sits in a black Syrian caftan on his pile of kilim like the lord of the manor. He is visibly pleased with the transaction. He solves Sudoku and crossword puzzles. "I was always good at math. I've been doing this for thirty years. It forms and trains the mind. I know every city in the world. Just ask!" Where had he been around the world? "In Iraq and in Saudi Arabia on the Hac. But I know every city in the world." Our merchandise is in the shop that belongs to his son, who would be packing it up, and he sends us off.

The son has obviously made something of himself. He has a shop with a store window on a busy street. He has a work desk with an armchair behind it and two armchairs in front of it; the carpets hang prominently from bars on the walls; they surrender their secrets, if they have one, regardless, without requiring the eye of the beholder to look for them. Whereas the father offers his pieces one at a time and the eye goes from one wonder to another in amazement. The son has many deep acne scars on his cheeks; they look like lost marks from the Arabic script which no longer know whether they once represented vowels or consonants. The packages are sealed, addressed, and taken to the post office next door. Insh 'Allah

– they may reach their destination. We pay him for the bill, not his father.

At tea he is talkative. "Yesterday there was a Dutchman in the city, who walked past my shop twice." (I had also noticed the Dutchman, because he scowled and gave the impression that he thought he was among thieves.) "The Dutch are cold-hearted, stingy and arrogant. Like the Norwegians and the Swedes. All northerners are like that. Miserly, and they don't buy anything. Americans buy everything. But we have not seen any here in a few years." The Italians and the French did not buy anything either, but at least they were warmhearted and friendly. "It's the power of the sun." Politely, he makes no mention of Germans.

We begin to talk about the Armenians. "Yes, we lived together well, Turks, Armenians, Jews, Christians and other nationalities, until the French came." (After the First World War England, Italy, Greece and France, divided Turkey into mandated territories; Anatolia had fallen to France.) "And the French have turned the Jews and Armenians against the Turks. Minority rights. You know what I mean. The Armenians succumbed, but not the Jews. That is why there are problems." I mention the massacre of the Armenians. "That was because of the war. It was completely normal. The talk about the massacres is nothing more than propaganda." I state my objections. Doesn't he know anything about the camps on the outskirts of Urfa, where the columns of refugees were gathered together to march in the Syrian desert? He brushes it aside. "What else!

What rules the world? Money. And who has the money? The Americans, Jews and Armenians. The Armenians still have their connections in the world. They are the richest of all. And with money you can also purchase history and rewrite history, and all the documents that come with it. It's that simple." Of course, personally he does not hate anybody. "We are all brothers."

Wednesday, 26 March 2008

To the grotto of Ayyub's birth, in the city where he sat, suffering and scratching the sores on his body, scorned by his wife. ("Curse God and die.") Under the ground. In the low-ceilinged room women sit and pray. A young woman has a small child in her arms. The child has been sick from birth, cannot stand up or run. She comes from the village and she was here to see the doctor, but he cannot help the child. Now she sits here and hopes for help from the Prophet. Later we see them out at the healing spring with a digital camera. Not far off there is a whole range of healing waters in plastic containers.

We aim for Nimrod's summer fortress, high up in the mountains. (Nemrut/Nimrod, the hero and the wanderer; the founder of great empires of the Euphrates and Tigris; the builder of the Tower of Babel; the founder of Nineveh, the sinful city that Jonah wanted to destroy; immortalised in the winter sky as the hunter Orion, which others see as Heracles.) We ask a man for directions. He begins to explain; a second man comes and contradicts him. A third contradicts the second, a fourth the third. There comes a fifth and sixth, who quarrel among themselves and point in different directions. Eventually, they seem to agree on the direction at least, but we knew that already. We only wanted to know which road to take up to it. But the road is poor. No, there is no road at all. And then the dispute begins anew. What is a road?

Osman, our driver, artfully wends the little Opel up the steep goat track at a walking pace. All the same, stones pound the chassis, and when the car began to skid he let it roll down the slope. From time to time, large cavities cut into the rock appear, like amphitheatres, equipped with giant horizontal and vertical stair-shaped stone slabs – stairs for the giants from Nimrod's entourage, or seats for them during the evening conversation about planned raids. Eventually it is too difficult for Osman's car, and we climb up the considerable distance that remains on foot, with panoramic views of the mountain landscape and up to Urfa, over the tracks of the sheep and goats, past a black-haired shepherd wearing a keffiyeh, and finally, to the top of the sprawling ruins of the giants, who once wanted to throw Abraham into the fire from a catapult. A giant archway has been preserved, constructed of large blocks without mortar, and beneath it there are smaller arches, four side by side, with a cuneiform, equilateral carved stone between them to hold them in place. Earth and stones lie haphazardly scattered around the base of the arches, so there must be a large, unexcavated room below.

While we balance on the stones and puzzle over the site, the governor calls and asks how things are going. Şenay tells him where we are. He has never been up here, but found the description so inspiring that he wants to drive up soon.

"But first you must build a road."

"I'll try. And if you want to come to tea again ..."

Nearby there are more of those stairs for giants and, at the centre, a room with an altar stone that has pools of water on the sides and a trough for the blood. Surely one of the many moon or sun temples in the region? Again we believe we can feel the breath of early history.

(All wrong. Later at the hotel Şenay calls an archaeologist: Nimrod's summer fortress was actually a monastery in the second/third century – Jacob's Monastery – named after one of the early patriarchs. There had been nine hundred thousand believers here in early Christendom, who were then forced to convert, were enslaved or slaughtered by the Bedouin hordes of Muslims in the seventh/eighth century. Eight hundred monasteries ... The giant stairs were discarded flagstones from the many quarries in the mountains. Is it a temple? But with the blood trough, what else could it be? He cannot explain. Oh, if only she had not asked him.)

During our descent a shepherd accompanied us until we reached a patch of grass, where his brother and his small son brought his lunch up to him. Water. Bread, tomatoes, olives, and goat's cheese. He invites us, as is the Anatolian custom, to share the meal with him, but we refuse – he would not have much left of this meagre meal for himself.

Among the few small plants that the sheep and goats subsist

34

on, I notice that there is a larger one I do not know: long narrow lush leaves that grow out of the ground, a single shriveled stalk in the middle with the flowers from the previous year. Cirisotu. Its leaves and flowers are poisonous, the root will be used as glue for the soles of shoes. Popularly known as Elias-Hesen-Stab: Hesen was the Koranic equivalent of Hermes/Mercury, the spiritual guide. Later the botanical name is provided: "asphodelus aestivus", the Summer Asphodele. Persephone would have brought it with her to commemorate her husband.

I sit on a rock and watch two butterflies, the only ones to date, one a common blue, and a swallowtail that pushes the wind in front of itself, surrendering to courtship. The wind, constantly blowing everywhere here, in the mountains, in the valleys, in the city.

Sitting on the rubble of civilisations, I see how carelessly we have trampled the rocks, the plants, the butterflies, that were there even before us and will remain after us. They too have a history, one calculated differently. They did not exist once and some day they will no longer exist; even the stones have changed in hundreds of thousands of years and continue to change. Only the wind has always existed and will always exist, even beyond our forever.

In the afternoon to the old shoemaker Ahmed in the bazaar. He sits hunched over a shoe – white beard, small brown crocheted cap, strong eyeglasses, the edges of which his shrewd eyes sometimes searchingly peer over – and pierces holes into the too hard sole with the awl. He must moisten them with

35

water in order to pull the thread through the upper part of the leather. Stitch by stitch. He works and he does not provide tea as a prelude to business. He makes three pairs of shoes now each day; in former times it was five times as many, but now he is 79 years old. What else should he do other than work, besides keeping himself healthy? Always the same shoes: buffalo leather for the sole, upper leather from cows, sheepskin interior, and between the soles soil, 'to discharge electricity'. In former times he worked many years for his master, but for fifty years he has had his own business, and here he sits. When he looks up, he turns his gaze two or three yards to the left into the next alley, or straight across to the business opposite. On the right the view is blocked by shoes. But he does not look up, or when he does it is fleeting, and the question is whether he wants to notice something from the tide of the eternal sameness that passes by him in two directions. For fifty years. The buffalo sole is still too hard and he cannot pierce it in with the awl. He must let it soften overnight. But no, now he has made it to the top, where the sole is thinner. "My shoes are comfortable, firm, and soft at the same time," – he does not say "the best" like a merchant – even dancers would buy them. Would we like to try them, just to feel them?

It is now one o'clock in the morning, so quiet that I can hear the Turkish flag, almost directly under the bright, waning moon, crackling in the cold north wind from the opposite mountain, the Nemrut Dağ.

Thursday, 27 March 2008

Down the narrow winding road from the hotel up to the Sultan Saladin Mosque. It is closed, but Şenay obtained the key somewhere. The mosque was an Aramaic church, built in 457, so it is one of the oldest. It was a church for eight hundred years, until it was rededicated by Saladin. A very high room, three naves, barrel vault and above the aisles and in the sanctuary, five columns lead from the pronaos towards the east. Through the emptiness of the space, covered with only a single, solid color carpet, its well-proportioned monumentality is to some extent merely to be sensed. There is nothing to distract – no altar, no images and pews, no confession stalls, no candles, no people. There is just the silent empty space, leaving you awestruck at the art of the early master builders to be able to create such great silence. The Muslims must have sensed it too, because almost unobtrusively, discreetly, the mihrab, the prayer niche for the Imam, is embedded in the south wall, with only the name of Allah and Muhammad in enchanting calligraphy above it, and next to the sleek mimbar is the staircase for Friday prayers. There is nothing demonstrative. Respect for the silence.

Nearby is a cemetery on a sloping plot of land. The dead are buried very close together, like the Jewish tradition. You cannot indulge in mourning among the graves. There are two high, flat stones on each grave: one at the head and one at the foot. The headstones on the graves of the older men are still crowned with a turban or fez. (Both were banned by Ataturk.) Some gravestones are completely green, painted in the colour of the Prophet, the sign of a godly man, who is readily called prophet in Urfa. Down the steep single cemetery road two young men on motorbikes travel, honking.

Through the humble, clean streets of the old town, up and down. In front of some doors there is garbage, tied-up in plastic bags. Şenay explains that food waste would never be put into the bags, but would be placed next to them for the animals or so that poor people could take it for their cats and dogs. To reach the Yeni Firfirli Camii, a mosque that was once the Armenian Church of the Twelve Apostles, we have to walk down an alleyway which is being dug up to lay water pipes, balancing on muddy stones in the hope we will not slip into the pit. I continue to sit in front of the façade while Şenay, again balancing over the water ditch, tries to find the key somewhere. On the façade above, there are heart-shaped windows built of stone between the pointed arches, which run down in ornamental drops. The individual droplets were sacred at one time, when water was scarce. So the drops are like chiseled gems.

Şenay has found the key at a greengrocer's shop and we can go inside the mosque. We are again confronted with this overwhelming sense of space – this time the nave is domed in quadruplicate; the third, upper dome, consists only of a circle of windows, so the very large space is illuminated everywhere and not one dimly lit, mystical corner remains. Now there is a bright, hyper-real silence. There should be some wonderful antonym for 'dead silent'. Silence and light in a room removed from time.

Friday, 28 March 2008

Not enough that five times a day and night blasting loudspeakers rip through the air with bloodcurdling sounds, which remind me every time of the wailing sirens of childhood, so that I flinch when they begin. The sounds are produced by men in cubbyholes in front of microphones, unless a tape is played instead. No one climbs up the narrow spiral staircases of the minarets – the loudspeakers are hanging there – and calls prayers in the four points of the compass anymore: "Whoever has ears to hear, let him hear." As if this was not enough, around noon today even the Friday sermon envelops the city of the prophets like the clamour of a gigantic alarm bell. That is acoustic terror. Which I am also acquainted with from childhood. Doesn't anybody actually complain about this ongoing noise pollution? The sacred surely cannot be so loud. Except for the Apocalypse.

To afternoon prayer in the small Ulu Cami, the Grand Mosque. It, too, was once a church – three naves, very low this time, thick masonry, square pillars – said to have been a synagogue before that, but there is no evidence. Scattered around the room, small groups of old men sit on the floor leaning against the pillars or the walls, looking forward. One at a time, younger men also come and perform silent prayer. Slowly the mosque fills with the faithful, who kneel side by side in rows on the north wall left and right of the mihrab. Everyone seems to pray at his own pace. After prayers, the Imam, who had earlier prayed for himself standing by a column, goes to the mihrab, kneels and begins to sing a sura, so I can *hear* the Koran with its monotonous, minimal-music-like melisma and rhythms for the first time. I listen to the strange sounds, fascinated.

From the group of men I took to be beggars, a blind old man who is pushed forwards to the mihrab rises and kneels beside the Imam. When the Imam has finished and leaves the mosque, the blind man slips into his place and begins to sing. It grows completely quiet in the mosque. No one steals away; everyone continues to kneel, spellbound. The blind man sings and sings with a deep dark voice that resounds in the sound-board of his body and the sound waves travel through our bodies like those from a gong. I no longer watch, am no longer curious about the unfamiliar; I can only hear and feel. It is as if the voice, like yesterday in the flood of light, is the manifest form of silence and exists outside of time.

On the way out, as the spell is broken, a mosque attendant dabs fragrance on the back of each person's hand. Muhammad is said to have praised Allah for three things: for the Koran, for women, and for fragrances. I would have added: and for the human voice.

Outside the hotel there is a little boy who wants to tell us the story of Ibrahim.

A hazy moon in the east, which barely makes it over the horizon.

Saturday, 29 March 2008

I climb up Nemrut Mountain in order to write, and sit down on a rock near the catapult. I did not know that there is also such a thing as Mother or Father's Day in the lower part of Anatolia. A good many family groups, ten to twelve people, are able to barbecue or picnic in the low area. In front of one group a boy stands and chatters the story of Ibrahim. Apparently children are trained – for strangers, for people from the villages – to learn the story and recite it. The family members clap in admiration; the father takes a photograph with the digital camera. I move on to the furthest end of the mountain plateau. Strong cold wind from various directions.

In the afternoon we travel through narrow, for the most part dark, impassable back roads, uphill, downhill. On occasion small shops tucked in among the walls of the houses – fruits, vegetables, drinks, plastic toys – but there is no one passing who wants to buy anything. I sit in the oblong courtyard of the Ulu Cami. Blossoming mulberry trees, male and female. Behind me in the cemetery boys play football. Women with large bags come out of the clothing market. I watch a man who has spread his prayer rug on the outer wall of the mosque and performs the normal physical rituals. I notice for the first time that, while standing, he bobs his head several times to the right and left – he greets the two guardian angels on his shoulders, then nods twice vigorously toward Mecca.

At dawn, on the terrace, I watch the birds. Flocks of brown doves hurry from left to right, from right to left, sometimes flying in a circular formation, sometimes dispersing in an irregular line, until they form a circle again. Are these obtrusive strokes before my eyes meant specifically for me to read? In order to do this, it is necessary first to delimit the space. I choose the Turkish flag pole on the opposite side of Nemrut Mountain as the left boundary and a high street lamp as a right boundary, as the temenos. Those that fly within the temenos 'count', those that fly outside do not count. Remarkable: since I set the boundaries of the oracle, the flocks turn, just before the marker, and fly off in the opposite direction. This can also be seen as a sign: search within yourself, if you want to know something.

Sunday, 30 March 2008

During my now nearly two weeks in Urfa I have read *The Black Book* by Orhan Pamuk. The game of deciphering the world came to me at just the right time: this method that is in the end equally criminal as poetic, although he does not mention it, is that everything points to something else and wants to be deciphered in its underlying second, third, and fourth meaning. During the trips across the country there were often signs on the road, on which one could read in capital letters 'Pamuk'. Admittedly, I knew that meant 'cotton', but I also 'knew' that it was an instruction and that it meant 'continue reading'.

The two narrators of *The Black Book* say that the world is full of symbols, which can be further reduced to letters, because that is where they come from. Letters can be found in nature, in the flight of birds, in the plans of cities, architecture, and on the faces of people. It is clear that this is not about the abstract Western alphabet (although the English word 'character' for letter is still a lingering reminder of the once magical significance of the Latin alphabet). It is the shape of the Arabic characters that is meant here, and I would also add the Hebrew. That a thing is thinkable, has to do with 'knowledge', that the original text of the Koran is in heaven – or that God looked into his Torah and then knew how he had to create the world. The symbols, these characters, are overt, but for the 'ordinary people' in Pamuk's Istanbul they are no longer readable, since with Atatürk's language reforms the Arabic was replaced by the Latin alphabet. But he could not extinguish the old and ever renewed symbols of the things and people inscribed. Pamuk's narrators read the calligraphic jumble of letters on the foreheads.

When the Westerner stares at the name of Allah, he is startled by the vertical command stroke of the Elif (the A), and affected by the little squiggle, like a pinched zero, like something crawling, which begins the name of Muhammad and by which in the shape of the letters the relationship of both is identified. The letters can be found again in the standing of the faithful at prayer and in the elongated posterior at prostration. They are found again in the domineering wrinkles of the forehead and the puffiness of the face. The zero, this mysterious figure that is written in Arabic as a dot, can collapse itself completely and can expand itself broadly. I see in the skywriting created by the

43

squadron of doves, the birds of the Prophet, the circles expanding and shrinking again. Since I have defined a temenos, they no longer come into the unbeliever's field of vision.

But what, other than the hidden coherence of the world, do the symbols in the novel mean? A secret account of a second coming, a new Mahdi, who will knock down everything that exists in order to build a new world. (The Islamic Mahdi were always power-hungry politicians, different from 'our' versions of the Antichrist or the Messiah. Their victories justified caliphates.) There is talk of a possible new military coup (the novel was written between 1985 and 1989). But how much real political expectations come into play here, remains to be seen.

As I read the book, almost two decades after its creation, there are again rumours of a 'coming' that is brewing in secret. There are enough 'signs,' like the interrogation of Ilham Selcyks, the imprisonment of the 'left' or the fear of demonstrations. Is a new 'father of Turkey' awaited? By whom? By the Kemalists? By the traditionalists? By the Islamists? That Pamuk and other writers can still be prosecuted for political expression – the 'honour' of disparaging Turkey – is certainly a sign that conditions cannot remain as they are. Allah as the frontal lobe and the flight of the Prophet's dove notwithstanding.

But the earth has me once more, faster than expected. In the afternoon I climb up the mountain in front of the castle again, because I never saw any people there from my window. Steep uphill climb through debris, no path, goat tracks. A small group of five or six young men try to climb the outside of the wall. I walked on and sat down on a rock. Two of the young men followed me, talked to me and pointed to a cigarette butt on the ground which they picked up. I understood, offered the first one a cigarette and then the second one, who took four or five from the pack – for friends, as I understood. And then they also came. The one in the orange-coloured sweater hung back a bit, sat down on the ground and played with a long folding knife. Then he came forward slowly. One showed me a slingshot and told me to shoot it. I had a queasy feeling and refused. The one in the orange sweater sat very close to me, while the other one was still waving the slingshot. The one in the orange sweater stood up again, briefly disappeared behind the rock and walked away with open hands. The others followed. I reached into my jacket pocket – my phone was gone. I shouted after the last one, the slowest one, the one with the five cigarettes, the word 'Handy' in various languages. He said "Tamam", which means something like 'All right', 'Okay', 'Don't get yourself so upset.' Should I run after the guys and demand that the one in the orange sweater give it back? He had already shown me his knife.

Şenay called the police, who wanted to send civilian policemen to the area immediately. I called home to have the cell phone blocked. In the depot there was already a policeman waiting, who took up the case. A second policeman came and I had to report the events once again. "Our beautiful Urfa. Nothing like this has ever happened here on the mountain, and not to a stranger, a guest!" A third and fourth policeman came in, including the Commissioner, and I reported the events again from the beginning. (They called my phone number, but it was already deactivated – "The party is not answering at this time". They had probably already taken the smart card.) A fifth officer drove the police car we used to leave the mountain and the village behind. Sometimes they asked children whether they had seen anything. A boy had seen 'the uncle' steal the cell phone and two fellows stormed down the mountain. No, it was not like that. A spot at the cemetery, where I had been yesterday, was apparently the transfer point for stolen goods. Nothing. A fellow took out his knife. We continue along the only village road, which is so narrow that the broad police car just barely made it through. The children and the adults are friendly, but no one had seen anything. I peered into every alley, every business, every open door – no orange sweater. Then down into the city, at a snail's pace past the countless phone stores, looking up and down the streets. Not a single orange sweater.

Then, far out of the city to the High Commissioner for crime, to look at pictures on the computer screen – about a thousand: men, women, juveniles, from 15 to 25 years old. Beautiful faces, melancholy faces, sly faces. A conspicuous number with protruding ears. "Are they really all criminals?" I ask after the five hundredth image. "No, no. They are all mixed together. Many are traffic offenders, some have applied for a residence permit." I see. But with fingerprints. Finally, after the thousandth picture, I can no longer tell them apart and say "Stop". I have taken note of five faces. Three are respectable citizens, one is a murderer who is already behind bars, the fifth had once stolen something, but that was six years ago. So again, nothing. To the eight or nine officers, who have been most friendly, making constant calls for the civilian police, worrying about my poor cell phone, the situation is visibly uncomfortable. "Our beautiful Urfa! How could this happen! To a guest!" They promise to pursue the case.

Monday, 31 March 2008

From the terrace I scan the long mountain slope with binoculars for motion, fixated on orange, because I think that is his trademark, and he probably has nothing else to change into. In the afternoon Osman, Şenay and I drive down the streets of the village again. I see that the deep chasm between the village and mountain where I saw them go, skirts around the entire mountain, and only surfaces again at the point in front of the cemetery which is the transfer point for stolen goods. I point out the place where I sat with the gang. The rock where the one in the orange sweater went to hide the phone in his pants is clearly visible. If I had turned around, I would have seen what he was doing. But I was too busy trying to shake off the fellow with the slingshot. While I examine every little group seated on the mountain, Mr. Ibrahim, from the Ministry of Culture in Ankara, calls to express his deep regret – it sounds like an expression of condolence. It is inconceivable to him that such a thing could happen in Urfa, and he apologises on behalf of the Ministry. So much sympathy and concern is positively embarrassing to me. I imagine how a Turkish writer who is visiting Germany as a guest would fare. He would probably shrug. Blame himself. Even Claudia Hahn-Raabe at the Goethe-Institut in Istanbul calls while travelling and is saddened by the story. As the victim of a robbery I now suddenly feel like a VIP.

In the late afternoon I sit on the terrace again and observe. Once, I think I can make out a small group with someone in an orange sweater who has just taken a seat. I briefly put down the binoculars to get a cigarette. When I look again the group has disappeared, swallowed by the earth.

What would happen if: after a few days of fruitless searching, in a cemetery – like Orson Welles on the ferris wheel in the Vienna Prater – the guy in the orange sweater emerges from behind a tall grave stone with a shiny switchblade. "You pursue me and think I don't notice. You are so stupid. Riding through our village, where I know every crevice in the walls, in a police car so wide you have to be careful not to scrape the walls of the houses, and I watch you go by. You didn't even know that the path winds around the entire mountain and emerges again at the place where people exchange stolen goods. By the time you finally got there, your cheap gadget – that couldn't even take a photograph – had already changed hands. Then you stand on the terrace for hours and search the mountain. Do you think I had not seen you? It was you who could not see me. In reality, I've been watching you the whole time. Even in the streets, while you scoured the cell phone shops at a snail's pace, I was always on your heels. Even today, while you were snooping around with your buddies in the red Opel again, I've been watching you. You strutted around like someone whose honour has been stolen and who showcases the sites of his humiliation with a mixture of disgust and pride. This afternoon you almost caught me while I was sitting with my friends on the top of the cemetery wall. We could have continued to sit there and thumb our noses at you until you had reached the police through the interpreter, and they would have come toddling along through the village at a snail's pace. By then we would have been long gone.

But I did not want to begrudge you this glimmer of hope, so I said to my friends, 'Jump down immediately when he puts down the binoculars,' so you know that we can steal more than cell phones. But it goes against my honour that you still want to find me, and I have better things to do than to monitor you. Here, you know my knife. But you are too pathetic, and my badge of honour is too precious to sully with your cowardly blood. I'll let you run. Better watch out in the future. Insh' Allah."

Tuesday, 1 April 2008

Driving west through well-ordered, rolling land. The earth – brown, yellow, red, black – indicates geological diversity, mostly of volcanic origin. The pistachio trees among the green fields look frosty, like winter trees, although they are already blooming and putting forth leaves; but that cannot be seen from far away.

It is the spot where Xenophon probably crossed the Euphrates with the Greek army in the wake of Cyrus the Younger, and where he later, after the death of Cyrus, led the 'train of ten thousand,' embattled by constantly renewed enemies, back home across the Black Sea. (We had of course read the *Anabasis* in third form; now suddenly what was vaguely remembered is given shape.) Here he hunted the fleet-footed wild donkeys and ate their soft flesh, along with the tough flesh of the clumsy bustards.

In the town of Birecik, which is our goal, the young captain Moltke, as a military adviser in the General Staff of the Sublime Porte, had set up a camp in 1834 with four thousand tents for eight regiments to pull together against the Egyptians in Syria, and he was vexed by the tactical ignorance of the Turkish commander. In wonderfully vivid letters to his brother, which show Moltke was a great stylist, he described the area from a strategic standpoint. He also marked and mapped it, bringing to life humans, animals, plants, and stones. "What a pity that I do not have Daguerre's *camera obscura* here." It is fortunate for the reader that he did not.

A vague recollection comes to me in preparing for the journey back, sometimes fleetingly, something acquired by reading. The idea takes my breath away; this rocky outcrop, this cliff, this river would have preserved a trail of the gazes that Xenophon, that Moltke, cast on them.

But we have driven to Birecik by way of the bald ibis colony (Geronticus eremita, bald ibis). These birds were once legendary in North Africa and Europe, spreading as far as the Alps, but by the eighteenth century they seem to have died out. And if one of the rare specimens did appear, it was difficult to identify it – hoopoe, raven, chough, curlew or what? We know it now as an Ibisart: the Schopfibis, Anita Albus writes in her book about rare birds. For centuries they brooded here in Birecik in the crevices of the cliffs high above the Euphrates, beyond the reach of nest robbers. But then the cliffs were blasted away or built over, the pastures along the river dried up, and they were threatened with extinction. Now an artificial wall with hatcheries has been raised, and they are there again, a hundred birds. They winter in Egypt and come, it is said, on schedule, on 14 February, a day of celebration for the small town, as the return of spring. They sit in or on the nesting boxes, always two by two, (because they are monogamous), and they lay one to four eggs that they hatch together. There are large birds – I estimate: as big as ravens – which have black plumage flecked with turquoise and red that shines in the sun. The head is actually bald (bald ibis), with a single long protruding feather at the back, a plume. The vulture-like head, which is not very attractive, ends in an overly long, sickle-shaped curved beak, as if they had to forage for food through bottlenecks. "Tschuk, Tschuk. Dar, Dar." The way they crouched there, motionless, unearthly and spectral, as if from a time long past, squat, reminds me of Hauff's story 'Kalif Storch' and his vizier in illustrations from

51

childhood. Should I shout "Mutabor"? Anita Albus writes: "In the eyes of Muslims from Birecik ibises carry the souls of the dead with their iridescent plumage." In the tradition here it was the northern bald ibis, not the dove that brought Noah the olive branch. You might believe that, if you see them gliding in a long, wide, straight formation in the sky. Not the fluttering of doves. And Mount Ararat is not too far away, at least not for this line of birds here.

Birecik is located on the Euphrates, this fairy tale river from *A Thousand and One Nights*, which I am seeing for the first time today. It is very wide here, seems to lie tranquilly, reflecting, and rushes quickly by; the water is so clear and pure that you can see far to the bottom with its large, bright, round cut pebbles. There is no indication that it is used for travel or in any other way: it simply flows, like in the old days. After a quarter of an hour walk along the river, two old fishing boats lying moored in the water come into view. On the banks eucalyptus; several palm trees, among them wind-blown canola; purple flowering bindweed; a single red desert anemone.

In the small old fortified town – Moltke described the rock-hewn passages inside the mountain – which consists only of shops for everyday needs, tractors, cattle feed in one hundred kilogram sacks, blacksmith shops for picks and shovels, people stare at us, as if no stranger had ever lost his way here. On the Ulu Cami, which they have here, too, an old man takes off his shoes to pray. He wants to know where I come from. When he hears "Germany" he says: "Mannheim. Cement." He has not retained anything more from the language. He repeats over and over: "Mannheim. Cement," as if the two words embodied the entire index of the encyclopedia – pleasure, expectation, hope, disappointment, and in his eyes there is a conspiratorial glimmer: "I know what I'm talking about."

On the return trip we turn off at Sürüc, an ancient Christian city that was once called Batnai and is located on the highway from Babylon to Edessa in the west, at the Syrian border. It is all a restricted military area, wasteland, secured by a barbed wire fence. A soldier explains to us that we should not drive close to the border. They might be using live ammunition. But on the Syrian side – we see it – the incomplete, newly built settlements extend to the border. Who is afraid of whom?

In the late afternoon the sky is in turmoil. Low, multicoloured clouds rush by above us. To the west, an ink-black front is forming.

Erdogan's ruling party faces a constitutional challenge because of increasing Islamisation. The continuation of Pamuk's *Black Book*? The party should be banned and its members excluded for life from political activity.

Wednesday, 2 April 2008
With the feminist Handan, in her office for the prevention of violence. Why does she wear the headscarf in the street? Out of solidarity. As a devout Muslim one could be free and independent. It is not about the headscarf: each person could do as she wished. In her classes, each containing ten women – none

53

of whom are likely to be related or come from the same village – the goal is to learn how they could detect and combat violence and verbal abuse, and defend themselves. Are there still forced marriages and honour killings? Certainly, but much less than before, and if so, it is in the villages, although even there the schools have done much to provide education. Here in the city the women are free, could do what they wanted, go out alone, go shopping, drive a taxi. In many of the families who stayed behind in Germany things are different. These married girls and young women in Germany are not allowed to leave the house (or if so, only when accompanied by their mother); they are not allowed to learn the language; they have no rights and no passport. If those girls between 16 and 18 years old who were born in Germany, grew up there and can speak the language well, had a German boyfriend, they would be shipped to an Anatolian village, would be married to a relative there regardless of how old they were, and, barely able to speak Turkish, without a passport, would never come out again.

I ask about the Kurds. Here in the city there are no problems, but they exist in the East because of the PKK. She talks about a family in a Kurdish village. During the night people from the PKK had come with guns and wanted to take one of the sons. When the mother resisted, she was beaten with a rifle butt and they indicated that if she resisted further, they would shoot her whole family. Then they went off with the boy. This happened again and again. Boys 6 to 10 years old would be taken away from their families, subjected to brainwashing and trained to be PKK militants. All done with the knowledge and approval of the Americans. The people from the PKK had American weapons. The Americans have an interest in destabilising the border area with Iraq, to then intervene as the 'savior' and establish bases. The PKK were notified about every movement via satellite.*

At noon, in the shop of a Kurdish felt maker, an old man. No, the workshop is somewhere else, but he tells us how felt is made. In the process, he tells us how it was invented. Seven hundred years ago a mystic – Hallac-i Mansur, at first a Christian, then a convert to the true faith – wanted to make something for shepherds that moisture could not penetrate.

---

* I do not know how old the Kurdish problem is, just that it did not start with Atatürk's ban on the Kurdish language. In his letters from Turkey, Moltke describes the composition of the Ottoman army before the defeat at Nisib: "There was such a horrible mortality rate that we have buried half the infantry during the length of our presence here. All the reserves are now almost exclusively in Kurdistan. The inhabitants of the village communities have fled to the mountains. They were hunted with dogs; those captured, often children and cripples, were tied to a long rope and led away with their hands bound. These soldiers, who did not even understand the language of their officers, had to be continually treated as prisoners. Tight sentry lines surrounded the encampment of each regiment, but often the guards themselves escaped. They paid 20, and later 100 florins for each deserter, but they were not able to prevent runaways. There were examples where 50 men with horses and weapons deserted the outposts. The soldier was well-paid, well-dressed, fed and treated leniently; but almost no Kurd endured it for more than two years; he went to the hospital, died, or ran away."

He had just shorn the brand new, freshly grown wool from the sheep, raked it out in order to distribute it evenly (he points to the tool), stamped his feet, raked again, then with a heavy wooden mallet (he points to it) he beat it flatly and firmly. But the stuff did not stick together, even though he repeated the process many, many times. He broke out in tears and his tears flowed on the stuff. The next morning, he saw that everywhere the tears fell, the material had solidified. Now he realised that water was the secret of felting. Salt water? No, simple, clear water. Incidentally, the mystic was later skinned alive by the Persian Sultan because he assumed to be God. The old man came from a Kurdish village. His father had owned a few fields, but he and the mother died young. But then the Ağa, the land-lord, had taken the fields from him and his siblings and chased them away. So they came here and learned trades. They were bad, the Ağas. They ruled over large clans and still have power over the small farmers. "If the Ağa found me he could, indeed he must, by his own law, kill me." Yes, but wouldn't there be Kurds in the Turkish Parliament? Yes, but these Kurds are all Ağas or sons of Ağas.

He wants to sell me a thick sheep's wool felt – "For the pasture, because no moisture can get through." But it is too heavy for me. Besides, I do not have a pasture.

Thursday, 3 April 2008
We travel once again to the planet sanctuaries at Sumatar. The day is sunny and cloudless; everywhere it is green in the Fertile

Crescent. On the mountains I notice the horizontal stratification. Because of road work, the signs everywhere have been taken down and we have to ask several times how to find the small turnoff to Sumatar.

In the village we look for the most distant mountain – the survey map is not clear – to find Saturn. The ascent over rock and karst takes about one and a half hours. Sometimes we lose sight of the goal and then we tell ourselves: just always keep the sun at your back. In the rock there are circular holes the width of three hands, either full of rainwater or fresh green vegetation with yellow flowers. On the rocks there is a blue-grey paper-thin moss that cracks under the sun, curling and scabbed like a wound. A dung beetle with a grey plaid mantle; another striped. When I pick one up, he crawls at first from hand to hand and then bites once firmly. The rocks have been polished down over thousands of years, sanded smooth, from the seemingly non-stop, cold and boisterous wind that blows here. We reach the top but find no sanctuary, only a mighty mound of boulders. So we are probably on the wrong mountain.

From here, however, with binoculars, you can make out a summit not too far away and the remains of walls that could not be seen from the village. So we go down and up again with the constant, fierce wind. A lizard in camouflage: I almost did not see it. Above us – "That must be Saturn!" – the remains of a circular ruin, probably a tower for stargazing. Fluted keystones lie on the ground below, the access to the interior is clearly visible, but filled in. Slightly lower in front of the tower there is a place of sacrifice with an altar stone and a blood gutter. From up here you have a panoramic view of the other planet mountains. It is hard to imagine the cult of the Sabeans: how can such an expansive landscape serve 'playfully' as a place of worship? From the main sanctuary to the Sin and Shamash temple in the middle, which I took on our first visit to be the sun temple, they may have been walking together down and up the hill to each sanctuary in succession, each named for the days of the week: Moon Day, Mars Day, Mercury Day, Jupiter Day, Venus Day, Saturn Day, Sun Day. They must have been unusually wide processions, but I can find no trace of the processional paths. Or else they had priests sit on every mountain, who observed 'their' planet and under certain constellations or perigees organised sacrificial festivals perhaps accompanied to the main sanctuary by their sacrifices.

From Saturn we descend, and then back up to the Sun Mountain: the same round site. From the Sun down and back up to Jupiter; always the same. Slightly deeper, closer to the village, is Venus, which we also want to climb, so once again down, and once again up. The paths drag on; we scramble up the fifth mountain. Again the same construction, in slightly better condition, but also without any access to the interior. Above, the guard is waiting, wearing a black suit like the one the other day. Nor does he know which mountain is which, contradicts us, and then, waving his arms, says no, there was really nothing left of Mars and Mercury, and Moon Hill is perhaps there or there or there. Furthermore, nobody climbs these mountains anyway, only madmen like the two Americans who came every summer for forty years, climbed up, climbed down, and then left.

We go down to the village with the guard, get the lunch box from the car and climb up to the main sanctuary in order to fortify ourselves in the shade of Shamash, sheltered a little from the wind. As a surprise, Şenay has brought along his thermos with delicious, chilled, slightly resinous wine. A young man in a business suit approaches; he is a bus driver, waiting for the children. He is from the village, had grown up here; he asks us why we are here. He has never heard of the planet sanctuaries.

In the distance there are herds of sheep and goats that are promptly converting the fresh, newly living seedlings from one state of matter to another. When a cow lows, we realise just how absolutely quiet it is up here when the wind grows once again still. From the village, far below, we can clearly hear a child's voice in the silence. Perhaps the ensemble of mountains has an acoustic mystery that moved the Sabeans to build their sanctuaries here. We know nothing about the Sabeans except that they were Semites and had a highly developed culture. Or so one can read. But how do we know that, if there is no evidence?

Friday, 4 April 2008
Around noon the town is empty of men. The security bars of the stores are down; those who have no security bars leave their shops untended or simply place a footstool in front of

them. The city is full of women in their purple headscarves; full of children. The women now speak freely. In front of the mosques the men stand, squat or lie in rows, because there is no space inside. One has indeed taken off his shoes, but pushed his bike to the place of prayer. As I watch the constant up and down, back and forth of the men, I realise why I have never seen a gym or aerobics studio. You do not need them here. The benefits of religion for life...

In front of all the mosques there are cypress trees. It is the tree of the mystics: its branches do not project out; they grow inward.

Today, like almost every day, a cold, biting, vicious wind from all sides, which even the sun, though trying very hard, cannot fight. In any event, it blows upon the mountains and terraces, but also down in the city, the minute one leaves the sheltered bazaar, and paper and plastic bags swirl in front of it.

This evening, like almost every evening, there is folk music on three floors of the hotel, for the locals, not for tourists, who do not exist anyway. Everyone eats abundantly, probably because you cannot talk over the volume of the music anyway. The song they sing today as their first number is a song from Urfa called 'Nemrud's Daughter'. Against the wishes of her violent father she loved Ibrahim and tumbled into the fire with him. A 'Nemrud', I learn, is in the vernacular for a cold, heartless, violent man. A fiend. Like the local wind. Nemrud has no intention of being myth or history.

Saturday, 5 April 2008

At the stonemason's. Two old men sit on the ground by the roadside in white dust and cut stone blocks. They have drawn lines on the stone to mark what they have to chip away. Stones for a fountain. They work effortlessly with the broad-edged hammers as if they were small tools. When I lift one, I am almost brought to my knees. They work with millimetre precision, using a metal rod to measure, again and again. It is hard work. The younger men do not want to do it; it would be too exhausting. People no longer need such jobs today, where the work is performed with concrete. For fifty years they hewed stones; it will continue a few more years. You must understand something about geometry, even about arithmetic, one of the old men says, and swiftly involves us in his narrative with a trick: how can you multiply 85 by itself in a single calculation? It can only be done with numbers divisible by 5. What would I do? Şenay tells him that I am a Hodja, a teacher. Also a difficult profession, he says. A Hodja must not only know something, he must also be able to create something: a stone, a shoe, a picture or even a human being. Meanwhile, the other old man prepares the midday meal – down in the pit there is a tent-like crate – and they invite us to share the meal with them. But we tell them that we have to carry on. Next to the tent there are already finished stones for the first round fountain: one almost exactly like the other, but not quite, not like one cut by a machine. It reminds me of Thomas Hardy, in the sense that he is criticised because his iambic verse is not always regular. In his youth he had been a stone mason and church builder, and replied that his stones had always been almost equal one to the other: they must match; that was all.

In a palatial town house from the eighteenth century – with a men's area and apart from that a separate harem – the art school is housed. We head for the watercolour painters. The Hodja explains the old Ottoman art to us, which the Sultan women had invented. The water in the bowls: chalk-less, but with a glue-like additive, extracted from a certain plant ('foxtail'), so the colours remain on the surface and do not run together. To produce this water takes three days. The colours: no chemicals, only the natural colours of earth, stones, and plants. He pours powder on a marble slab, spread-ing it out with a marble stone (like a rolling pin) in eight sweeps: it would take hours – three, four – until the powder, bonded with chalk-free water, was mixed uniformly. Then the paint, with a few drops of ox bile added, is dropped with a horsehair brush into the water in the tub: it lies there and spreads out on the surface with clear contours. The Hodja now arranges it with a small stick and conjures up flowers and leaves from the self-forming ornaments, in the colours one always wants – pure white, pure red, green. The paper is spread over the surface, and then the singular, unrepeatable image is extracted.

The calligraphy master has just started the lesson. One at a time the girls – there seems to be almost only girls sitting in the classes – step up to his table to have their homework corrected. He does it with each girl's quill, so he can also examine whether or not the writing instrument has been properly sharpened. (During the first year the teacher always sharpens the reed.) "There is a resistance between the hand and the hard quill; when that is overcome, the script flows." He corrected very slowly, reconstructs the line, which is not round enough or too round, and the serif, which, as only a straight line without the slight curvature down, has failed. For the fine script he uses the thin quill pen ("From Persia: they have the best quill; it has to be young and at the same time very hard"); for wide strokes the short bamboo quill. The ink is made from the soot of burnt oil, bound with glue. He dips the quill into the ink pot, stuffed with a nylon stocking for lack of silk – so the quill takes only as much ink as it needs, and does not drip. The week-long papermaking class with onion skins used for the colour – no, that is really going too far, on and on, and finally we end up with the first draft of the Koran. How long would the calligraphy lessons last? Three years, with five to six hours of practice every day. He shows us the sample catalogue that must be learned. At the end there are marvelous characters of the highest abstract beauty. To create them you no longer need to be able to paint.

The silversmith workshop: tiny silver beads that are 'spun' into a gossamer thread. With his sausage fingers the master artfully bends the wire strands into delicate ornaments: birds' eyes, flowers, royal attributes that, when strung together, result in necklaces, bracelets, and earrings. If I look long enough, I'll be able to distinguish the junk from the artistry in the shop windows. But the younger generation no longer want to pursue his work. "Everything has to be cheap. Cheap. Cheap. It will be thrown away soon, anyway."

The last stop today: a course for stonework ornamentation. Again, almost exclusively girls and young women, squatting on the floor in white dust and chiseling floral patterns out of the water-softened Urfa stone. Off to the side sits a young blonde woman who speaks a completely pure, accent-free German. She was born in Berlin, went to school there until she was twelve, and then wanted – it is hardly possible to say "to return" – to Turkey, where her parents wanted to join her, but never arrived. She has now been in this country for twelve years, alone, finished school, became an English teacher and was then put for starters in the province for four years.

"In the villages it is only two years," I say.

"Yes, but in the provincial towns it is four. How do you like Urfa?"

"Good. Very good. Urfa is beautiful."

"Yes, everybody says that. Everybody who stops here briefly and then continues on. If you have to live here, you know how awful it is. There's nothing. Nothing at all. A few ruins which amaze the foreigners, hype about the prophets for the Persian pilgrims. Otherwise there are nothing but cell phone shops, the length of an entire block; dresses that are so ugly no one will wear them; inelegant, cheap shoes that pinch. Handicraft folklore and the corresponding music in the hotels. I cannot even go out here..."

"Because there is no disco?" I ask.

"No. No, even with my only friend here" – she crouches down across from us and chisels – "I cannot go into a cafe or a tea garden. People would give us nasty looks, as if we had done something forbidden." Does she think the class is fun? How could it be? There were sixty young people per class, aged 13 to 16 years old. The worst part of puberty. There was nothing she could do. The only thing to distract her somewhat from the desolate city, was being here chiseling stone. Do I like her ornaments? She has worked long and hard on them. "Yes. They are very, very lovely."

Monday, 7 April 2008

Once again high up to Göbekli Tepe, in the Stone Age. You can see more clearly than the first time: we drive through basalt fields, and at the foot of the excavated sanctuary there is flint everywhere, the material used for the tools and arrowheads of the Neolithic hunters. The air is very clear today in the biting wind, the view so vast that you can see the volcano which produced the rocks. There is a different guard today. With him is a black horse with white markings on its head which he is grooming. It turns out that he is not a guard, but the Ağa, the landlord. With a gesture of his hand he points in the cardinal directions: these are all his fields. Had he reached an agreement with the government on the purchase price? No. They were now negotiating on an exchange, land for land. He is one of five brothers, in whose name he negotiates. He is a clever farmer. Above, behind the wishing tree, he has planted olive groves on two sides. The trees bend beneath the wind, almost touching the ground. Between the trees there are eight girls in brightly coloured clothes, pulling up something green (euphorbia?) like fodder and stuffing it into bags. Later, they strap the heavy bags on their backs and carry them down to the village. Sometimes along the way they lie down with the bags to rest.

The Ağa walks with us to the fenced excavation site, and we look back down on the T-stelae, standing in a circle. They were nearly 5 metres high and no one knew, until now, how the T-bars had been hoisted so high. Through the binoculars I again see the animal representations and curved ornaments. Between two arches I see an animal with its head lifted so high that its horns touch its back. An antelope? The Ağa shows us a newly staked-out excavation site, spread open just along the edges. He points to one of the cornerstones on the ground. On them – as primitive as children's art when compared to the animal representations – you can see the outline of a prominent human head and chest. Was there a dread of illustrations or reliefs of people that dated back to different periods?

On the way down through the mutilated plants to the guard's hut, I see clusters of a knee-high plant that I do not know. Long stems with paired lateral shoots, where sprays of many tiny blue flowers have begun to bloom. The pale-green, lance-shaped leaves are covered on the top with small sharp spines. It is the only eye-catching plant in the otherwise meagre vegetation. I ask the Ağa what it is called. "I do not know them. All I know is that they are not edible." That illustrates the mind of the farmer, directed exclusively to what is digestible, what is useful. The Stone Age hunters probably did not think differently, when they decided to settle: not here, at any rate. For a sanctuary it was the same.

Tuesday, 8 April 2008

Once again to Harran, said to be a Sumerian or Akkadian name, which means 'caravan'. We pass through a wide, fertile plain. Where it is not yet green, the cotton will soon shoot up from the gleaming brown fields. In front of the city wall to the west lies the legendary watering hole, where Jacob saw Rachel for the first time, as she watered her sheep and goats. For seven years he served Laban, her father, for her hand, and then another seven, because the first time he got only the elder sister Lea, ten times more fertile, in fact, but bleary-eyed. It is easy to imagine that Laban needed an able shepherd in the vastness of the plain, especially considering the fact he served in vain because he was in love. One detail of the story was always a mystery to me: when Jacob finally wanders off with his wives and children and flocks, Rachel steals her father's portable idols. What kind of idols were they? Now I can base a verse on it: during the second millennium – therefore the time of the patriarchs – a Hittite and Mitanni king concluded a peace treaty here, in this already ancient city, in the name of the moon and the sun god, Sin and Shamash. Why should Laban renounce these powerful, highly visible gods, immortalised in stone, on the rumour of an invisible God, who had held out to Abraham the prospect of everything imaginable in the future? The prospect! In any event, they could not compete with temples and images and the adoration of the leaders of the world. And Rachel was probably skeptical and opposed to her husband Jacob's God. Does it mean something that 'Laban' was the name of the moon god in the region of Lebanon?*

Incidentally, the watering hole is unsurpassably dreadful: a spacious, walled square with two-metre-high flamed wrought iron grilles that only look pretentious and expensive. The square itself is littered with plastic bags and many years of waste. The watering hole, where two wells, now run dry, had once been dug, is covered with washed-out concrete. The memory of lovely Rachel has trickled away like the water that was once drawn here.

We drive around the city walls to the Baghdad Gate on the east, wandering through the fortress with its gigantic, brick vaults from the Byzantine period, on the way to the Trulli houses

---

* The fear of idols has long continued to have an effect. When in the Hebrew Bible God is compared to a rock, the Septuagint translated it to *force* or *power* (dynamis), to exclude the possibility that God could be worshiped as a rock, as was not uncommon in the religions of those maligned as idolaters. Later, when Jesus gave his disciple Simon the name Peter, rock, on which he would build his church, the fear was dispelled and replaced through an act of speech. Joyce commented that the church was founded on a pun.

past the iron loft beds which have already been set up outside; in summer people sleep outside, up high, not only because of the coolness, but also as protection against snakes and scorpions. In front of one of the houses, a man invites us into his courtyard. He owns a dozen Trulli houses, which are all connected together inside. A daughter immediately takes us inside, where there is an established business – the usual clothing and cloth bric-à-brac, copper kettles and pots, pitchers, and grandfather's pistols which must, upon closer inspection, have come from the Seven Years' War. Terzerole. God only knows how they found their way here. Maybe Kara Ben Nermi lost them. When the young woman realises that we do not want to buy anything, it does not matter. We sit down in the yard with the whole family. The daughters with black painted eyelids hand out tea; the father Ali rolls cigarettes and talks. He has five daughters – they laugh and beam at us – and five sons. The youngest son is still small. Ali is proud of his wife – she is 43 years old. She looks twice as old, but is cheerful and friendly like the daughters. He could only send one of the sons to school; there was not enough money for more. Then he asks us what we are doing, why we are here. He asks, comments; the daughters listen, smiling. Everyone seems to be truly interested in these funny strangers. Nobody thinks about business dealings anymore. When we want to pay for the tea, he makes it clear to us that this would insult him.

As we are leaving, we see a woman in a sequined dress in front of her mud house scrubbing the concrete 'terrace' with large quantities of water. Sometimes the shaft of light from a sequin catches our eye. In front of the 'terrace' there are two television satellite dishes in sand. Beside them, two old women are patching their mud house. They take lumps of clay from the ground, slap it on the wall and spread it by hand.

We eat lunch in the slender shade – the only shade far and wide – of the observation tower, which was once a minaret, which was once a church tower, which was once an astronomical observatory. It is 15 metres high, said to have been 30 metres high at one time. But the height is of no use to us – how quickly the earth turns, demonstrated by the number of times we have to move. A friendly guard allows us into the cordoned-off excavation site. You realise for the first time how monumental the site is when you inspect it, when you actually experience it physically, not when you only see it. Clearly visible now in the remains of the buildings or at least in outline are the mosque, the church and the temple procession corridor. Whatever else was layered over or under it at the time, now lies harmoniously side by side and bound together in space. "Here time becomes space."

In the evening, two likeable young reporters conduct an interview with me for the local television. No lights, no umbrellas, just a small digital hand-held camera. When I want to speak English, they say – studied young men – they cannot speak English. So we need Şenay's help again. I ask them about the bleakness of this city, because I remember the young woman from Germany I met a few days ago. About thirty years ago, they say, they had a happy life here. Down in the park, in

70

today's tea gardens, there was, as everywhere in the Western world, wine and beer, raki, belly dances. Nine cinemas in the city. Then suddenly everything had been – no, not forbidden, simply silently taken away. Only after years of massive pressure from the youth and the Liberals could at least *one* movie theater reopen. They argue, yes, Muhammad had forbidden alcohol. Without using the north and west of Turkey as an example to counter their argument, where of course alcohol is consumed, I suggest that they may rather, for once, ponder the idea in Urfa of vocalising the text of the Koran differently. There were just so many possibilities, those of critical scholars in exile and so on and so forth. Perhaps something else would be revealed and the Prophet had meant something else? No, if things are doubtful, it is better for things to remains unchanged.

Wednesday, 9 April 2008

A last visit to the Archaeological Museum. The Deputy Director will guide us. Again in front of the oldest human representation, the Urfa Man. I had memorised him at first sight. The arms hang down straight from the square shoulders, bending only at the elbow from the middle of the body, the fingertips touching above the visible phallus, next to the testicles. What I only now noticed, hanging from the neck, is an ornamental ribbon which tapers off at the breastbone. Hans Blumenberg once wrote that culture begins where man steps outside the original scheme of stimulus and response, where he takes a break, hesitates, thinks. Things that are unnecessary, non-functional, superfluous, are created (based on the survival of the species), but they satisfy another need, one that is ornamental, 'decorative', aesthetic, that comes from the combination of reflection and play. That is why – more so in the ribbon than the phallus and the testicles – the beginnings of culture can be found in Urfa Man.

The Deputy Director tells us what is now known about Göbekli Tepe: there are still 20 (!) more stone circles in the ground under the one excavated. Two pillars face south, the others by these two. Certainly it is not a settlement, "only" a temple; a shrine. These Stone Age people had not yet been settled, they were "a ceramic": that is, they produced no ceramics, although they existed "at the same time". They buried their sacred pillars in the earth themselves when they moved on, so other tribes could not find and destroy them. So here is this earthwork embankment! (By the way, Professor Schmidt, the excavator of Göbekli Tepe, arrived in the city yesterday.)

We say goodbye to the people we met in Urfa, to the extent that we can find them. To the ancient stonemasons who still sit in the same spot in the dust and smooth their stones. They want to make us tea and prepare a midday meal. To the old drum maker and lambskin finisher, to whom I will give slightly more than the little he charged and then wished me – inner and outer – wealth. To the Kilim dealer who suddenly shows up unexpectedly, because our presence was apparently drummed along through the bazaar from stand to stand, and who beseeches us to come to him yet again, because he has received a new shipment of the most beautiful kilims. And we say goodbye to the old shoemaker who wishes me a straight path with Allah, liquid-flowing like water, and without stones.

Istanbul, Friday, 11 April 2008

Yesterday, farewell to Urfa. One last little tour through the park with festively dressed people, the men in black harem pants, stiff-legged and dignified, walking at a clipped snail's pace as if they were carrying something precious; the women and children, dazzling and colourful, pass by, to Karpfenteich, to Nemrut Mountain. Fresh trays of sesame-coated bread rings, always on the minds of boys. Again and again Judas trees covered in blush-red. I photograph one of the most elaborate blossoms and later press it carefully into Pamuk's *Black Book*.

Evening flight to get here. On either side, miles and miles of lights from the giant city. From above you would have to describe this sea of houses, with its currents, depths, shoals and breakers, as if it was created by the lights. The waterways, however, are black, except where the spotlight of a ship crosses through them.

Şenay has the taxi driver take a detour, and so I see the Hagia Sophia, the Blue Mosque, and Topkapi for the first time by night. I had not imagined these mythical places were so monumental. From the window of my hotel on the side facing the Pera Museum, you can see the illuminated Hagia Sophia on the left; above the Golden Horn, very large, the crescent of the rising moon.

After breakfast, a short walk up a steep, stepped road. View over the Golden Horn to the silhouettes of the mosques. Below, between the noisy street to the hotel and the water, houses that criss-cross haphazardly, where it seems there was just barely enough space for them to be built. In between the beautiful old, mostly abandoned wooden houses that were once noble quarters and are now waiting for the torch. (I learn later that they were uninhabitable because of the vermin; if they were renovated they would still be uninhabitable because of the pesticides they would have to use.)

At half past ten Claudia Hahn-Raabe, director of the Goethe-Institut, picks me up at the hotel and we drive to the University, where I am received by a group of amiable German, English, and French-speaking members of the Faculty of Translation Studies. The 75th anniversary of the literature faculty is currently being celebrated in Istanbul, founded and organised by Leo Spitzer and Erich Auerbach. Lunch in a beautiful old university building. (No: I hear later that it was built as the War Department under the Ottomans.) Lecture on the problems of translation from non-Indo-European languages, or translation into those languages. In English. Most use headphones in order to follow along in Turkish.

Then we want to have a cup of tea and drive down – you must always go down or up in this city of what was once seven hills; now there are certainly seven times seventy – to an elongated square overlooking the Sultan Suleymaniye Mosque by the great architect Sinan, Mimar Sinan, of the sixteenth century. It is considered a masterpiece, and that it is. This is demonstrated by the first fleeting encounter. Behind the main entrance to the wide area I look up to the first dome, which is so high and perfect that it almost eludes the eye, or even comprehension. It floats, apparently without any support structure. Light, light. Unfortunately, the great room with the large dome cannot be seen. The walls are covered by scaffolding. The stone exterior, limestone, is of plain grey. The Mosque looks as compact and enclosed as a turtle. As if Allah had carried it down on his open hand and placed it here.

Later an appointment with Şenay. We talk about politics and the things that I – or any other stranger – have not noticed. She had already told me in Urfa that after my television appearance on the penultimate evening a group of Turkish German merchants wanted to invite me to dinner, which did not occur because we were leaving. She says now, throughout my time in Urfa there were requests for interviews from newspapers, radio and television, and she had always brushed them off, even up to one day before departure. "I wanted to protect you. Who knows who wanted to exploit what, what then perhaps a counter-group would have gotten on the agenda. It is dangerous, politically, to say something noticeable." She mentioned a little-known Turkish author who had spent a night in our hotel. The whole night the police had stood in front of the hotel. It is good that I did not find out such things until now. I would have moved less freely in the city and would have been perhaps more cautious with my questions. The large police presence because of my cell phone – was that petty little matter really the reason? I immerse myself in the secrets of calligraphy and the flight of the doves and the entire time I am a fly in the spider web. Or not. "Our beautiful Urfa ..."

Saturday, 12 April 2008

Brunch at the home of Claudia Hahn-Raabe. From her balcony, where the wisteria hangs already in heavy bunches, the eye goes to the water. The whole wide Marmara Sea lies at our feet; left and right, the mountainous district of two continents; in the distance in the haze, the Princes' Islands. A blessed piece – of what? You cannot call it earth; you cannot call it a landscape. Well then, *seascape*. Why don't we Germans have that word? (And you can only say 'blessed' if you do not know what slaughter took place here. At the moment the once powerful Orthodox monasteries on the Princes' Islands with their priceless libraries are crumbling down towards their debris.) Far below a cruise ship lies moored along the quay. The mirror-like surface of the water is flecked with the black of fishing boats in the April light, like those in a Chinese scroll painting. As a ferry cuts through the silence with a long diagonal line without disturbing the fishing boats, which sway almost imperceptibly from their spot in the distance.

I meet Şebnem İşigüzel, the young author who will come to Frankfurt in September for the Book Fair. She is very amiable, pretty, dainty, elegant, and it's hard to imagine that she wrote this novel about the underworld of Istanbul, brutal beyond all limits of endurance, which in Turkish is simply called *Trash* but in German is called *On the Edge*. Her husband, a respected landscape photographer, is Armenian, and she knows about many Armenian communities in Germany. When I rave to her about my discovery of the architect Sinan, she says: "You need to know that he was Armenian." An Oriental beauty with thick black ringlets, a dark voice, dark hair and dark eyes, very erotic, her ancestors came from Bulgaria, she talks in dazzling German about her studies of the Syrian 'oral tradition' in Mardin. She knows the congregation where I have been, and Father Gabriel. She has learned the complicated alphabet, but has difficulties with the vocalisation and therefore focuses on the oral tradition. We are talking about the long-term exposure, probably imperceptible because of the exaggerated separation, of cultures to each other (visible in certain prayer signs): has Islam influenced the Syrian rite or was it the other way around? I recall the importance of the Syrian Christians to Islam, reported by Father Gabriel. In which direction influences extend, of course, is hard to decide. To clarify that, it could only help to doubt religious (national, ethnic) 'identity'. I meet Dilman Murçadoğlu, who has translated my journal entries into Turkish and says how much she had liked reading them, always looking forward to the sequel, but also how difficult the translation was. She comes from a corner of the Black Sea in the direction of Georgia, where Luwian is spoken, an

Indo-European dialect from the Anatolian language family, written in Cyrillic. She still speaks it with her mother. When I imagine that Luwian was spoken in the Hittite empire and has survived for more than two and a half thousand years, the long breath of history shivers through me, quite different from the earlier excavated stones, which can no longer be brought to life. I think of the Bedouin language that derived from the Egyptian Pharaonic, or of the kilims, which have had the same patterns for centuries.

After brunch at Claudia's, I no longer know what Turkish is. ("I am proud to be a Turk!") It is obviously an imaginary measurement, a construct that was called into question by everyone I struck up a conversation with, including those in Urfa.

In the afternoon I had an appointment with Şenay at the Alman Fountain, but the taxi driver takes me to Ahmed Fountain (I know neither the one nor the other), directly at the entrance to Topkapi Palace. I wait. Directly in front of the Gate to Paradise, which I am not able to enter for the time being, because I am waiting. Buses and taxis drive up and unload visitors. Dozens. Hundreds. Again and again, other merchants want to sell me postcards, souvenirs, guides, city maps, sesame-coated bread rings. After an hour they give him up, this bystander or loiterer – surely he cannot wait for something for such a long time. Or maybe he can? But what for?

After another hour, I also give in and want to make at least one more dash – it is not far – to the Hagia Sophia, this architectural marvel, the centre of Eastern Christianity for a thousand years. The expectation is great, as is the disappointment. What stands there is no longer standing; rather, it lays there more like a hybrid shellfish, heavy, burdensome, repellent. Due to the lack of exterior plaster, the many renovations and additions are conspicuous. In later centuries (the church was consecrated in 537, after only five years of construction), enormous support structures were added, because the dome, unthinkably wide and high according to the notion of the times, collapsed repeatedly.

But when you enter, it is as if you are stepping out of our contingent, patched, crumbling world, its auxiliary constructions vulnerable, into a transcendental chamber, the revelation of an eternity. What appears to be cowering on the outside, withdrawn, is inside wide and light, as though you were now seeing face to face, clearly, what had before appeared only as if in a dark mirror. Because of the unevenly set stone tesserae, the mosaic of the Virgin and Child in the narthex flickers from step to step in the changing golden light like the stars in the desert night. Inside, everything is magnificent, powerful and of a monumentality that had no equal in our Roman Christianity. Eight of the high marble columns were transported here from the Artemision in Ephesus. The Great Goddess, from whom the apostle Paul was forced to flee, was a handmaiden to an even more cherished deity. The dome, 50 metres high, is surrounded by scaffolding, therefore I can sense more than I can see what is still left in the mosaics which represent the height of Ostrom's power. Nevertheless, walking through the halls and colonnades makes one feel very small, and it also shows that there was once a span, distance and majesty: the threshold of the church by the highest of the nine gates only the Emperor could cross. (The builder, the Emperor Justinian, once said proudly that with the Hagia Sophia, he had surpassed King Solomon's Temple.) Today we all trample through the Emperor's Gate, remaining a moment, at best, to snap a photograph of the height.

I walk down the road towards the Hippodrome and see a tall bronze column with the bodies of three snakes twined around one another. (At the hotel I read that it was the votive offering of the Greeks from Delphi, in gratitude for the victory over the Persians at Plataea.) I see the obelisk of Julian the Apostate, who was sent for from Heliopolis to try to stop Christianity. The short street is proving to be a true procession of religions: from Egypt to Delphi, to Ephesus, to the Roman Hippodrome after Ostrom. "Everywhere there are gods," wrote Thales. But that was referring to the road from Didyma to Miletus, and remained within the boundaries of ahistorical and cosmic time.

I want to walk back to the hotel – the taxi ride did not seem too far – and think I can go along the Sea of Marmara, the pinnacle of Topkapi behind me. To lose one's way in a city, Benjamin writes, requires some schooling. I have not learned it. I walk and walk, Turks grilling in the grass on my left, ships, port facilities; to my right the remains of the Ottoman city wall to protect against enemies who could come through the

Dardanelles by sea. I walk and walk, but there are no signs, Beyoğlu or Taksim Square, only a stream of cars in both directions from anywhere to anywhere, so that I cannot even cross the street. Eventually, after a half hour, I have a feeling I will never reach the Bosporus (actually there was no way for me to get there, as I realised later when I look at the map) and I hail a taxi. It drives halfway back, then takes a left turn, where there is actually a sign which reads: Taksim Square. But it is mounted only in one direction, and that is why I could not see it. I understand: to lose one's way requires schooling. The trip cuts right across the city, up through the enormous Roman aqueduct and down across the Galata Bridge, the anglers standing close together on both sides.

From the hotel I reach Şenay, who waited for me over three hours at another fountain. How the minutes and hours of waiting drag on, expand and spin out, how the two millennia from Tutmosis III to Justinian can skip by in twenty minutes.

A cloudy crescent high above the Golden Horn.

Sunday, 13 April 2008

The Oriental beauty, Ülker, picks me up at the hotel. She is the daughter of a German woman who is very revered here, Şara Sayin, who established the department at the old university, similar to Spitzer's and Auerbach's Romance studies. I met the sprightly old lady on the street yesterday or the day before. She looks and talks like a German, rotating herself in the process as if hopping from one side to another. A Northern European type. Quite different is her Oriental daughter. Her long black hair is tied back. Attentive and alert, yet at the same time a somewhat amused look in her black eyes. A trace of the form of melancholy meant by the word 'hüzün', which I still cannot quite apprehend. A wistful well-being? A permanent mourning for the lost glory of this city? Ülker has a book about the Korean communities in Germany in my area (Offenbach, Hanau, Gießen) with the names of the villages around Mardin where the members come from.

The posh brunch on the terrace of the Goethe-Institut has been organised for Michael Balhaus, the famous cameraman, who has been invited as chairman of a film jury. He talks about his curiosity about what those who have just arrived in Turkey are doing now. There's a young director whose film *My Father the Turk* has just met with success. The father had a wife and three daughters in an Anatolian village, went to Germany, had a son with a German woman, went back to his village to his wife ('the daughter-making machine') and the daughters, but wanted to take his son with him to educate in his own way, but the German woman refused. The son did not speak Turkish; the sisters do not speak German. The film is shaped by the strained inability to communicate, the insults, injuries, and incompatible mindsets – evidently with much wit.

I meet the constitutional expert who speaks German flawlessly and has accused Erdogan's party of a constitutional violation, wants to prohibit them and their members from all political activities for five years. He is a strict secularist and does not shake hands with a woman who is wearing a headscarf. He says that no one will go on holiday, in order to protest immediately if the Prime Minister does not quickly change the law (about immunity), which he could do. Dilman, who has just translated Habermas, asks me about a word from the constitutional law which she is not familiar with. I do not know it either and introduce her to the constitutional lawyer, who immediately refers her to her Turkish counterpart.

Then, with Claudia Hahn-Raabe to Topkapi Palace. The grounds are much smaller than expected, the building low. Hard to imagine that under Süleyman the Magnificent, who conquered not only the countries of the West, but also carted off their scholars, five universities once operated here. Glorious handicrafts, embroidered silk jackets, flags, weapons, especially the incomparable illuminated manuscripts, which require time for every single page. The beard of the Prophet, which you are not allowed to represent if you swear by the beard of the Prophet, is distributed across multiple engraved boxes. His turban must have perched on an elephant skull. There is also the rod of Moses, a thin, gold plated stick with the first signs of branches. Hard to imagine how he was able to strike the rock in Sumatar.

The short road down to the Blue Mosque, which I ignored yesterday. Giant dome that rests on five half-domes, which are in turn supported by arches on columns. The spatial impression of the mighty building (not by Sinan) seems like a sheer demonstration of power. Crowds of people standing around snapping pictures. The mosque is blue because of the Iznik tiles which can only be seen in the gallery. And apparently also to touch – the tiles are, depending on the colour, fired in different stages, and when you move your fingers over them you can feel the thickness. Perceptible presence of the production process.

By tram down over the Galata Bridge. Anglers, anglers, anglers – and up the next hill, then a stretch by foot further up to a fish restaurant, up on the terrace of a hotel, with views overlooking the Golden Horn in the hazy early evening light. The illuminated mosques, crouching or nesting like hemispheres above the sea of houses. The Hagia Sophia, the Sultan Ahmed, a few that I do not know, then the Süleymaniye of the great Sinan.

A sultry day. Now, about one o'clock, a gloomy crescent, like yesterday.

Monday, 14 April 2008

My last day. I walk once again over the bridge up the hill to the Süleymaniye Camii with its immeasurably wide complex. If you come from below, from the Horn, you first see the sloping terrain and get an idea of the technical knowledge, the need to stabilise the construction through deeper and deeper substructures. And the art is not to notice it as you would if the huge complex was on a vast plain. There are five schools up there on the square, a hospital, a public kitchen for the poor, the large courtyard with the fountain, the gigantic Cami off to the side, and the inaccessible tomb of Süleyman on the right. He wanted to have his master-builder with him in the tomb, but he refused and constructed a little grave for himself outside the complex, northwest in the diagonal to his master, toward the Golden Horn, the water, like a signature under his work, which should not be disturbed by its own earthliness.

I walk back down the mountain to the water. Just before the bridge a teenager walks past me quickly, carrying his shoeshine equipment. When he has passed me, I hear a clattering thud, turn around and see that he has lost his brush. I call after him; he comes back and seems happy to have it back. He shakes my hand effusively and wants to brush my shoes in gratitude. I fend him off. First, it was not worth mentioning; second, nothing can be done to Camper shoes with cream and a polishing brush anyway. But he asks, almost pleadingly, and I do not want to offend his honour, which requires that he pay thanks. He polishes for a minute or two, where there is nothing to polish. I thank him very much, and he says: "36 euros." What? "Yes, 18 per shoe."

In the evening, flight back to Frankfurt over the sparkling sea of houses and the black water.

Aegean Journal

Ayvalık/Cunda, Wednesday, 12 November 2008
Yesterday morning flight from Frankfurt to Istanbul. During the entire flight a self-contained cloud cover lay below us: old snow, seen from above on Lake Sils, criss-crossed by innumerable cross-country ski tracks. Sometimes a sparsely dusted mountain top, never a clear view down to the land.

In Istanbul Fügen Ugur from the Goethe-Institut picks me up and we meet Ülker Sayin, who I know from Istanbul and who will be accompanying me. Next flight with Ülker to Izmir. From there, two hours by car to the north, through a brown, hilly landscape with views of the blue quiet sea and small islands. Extensive olive tree plantations; under some of the trees there are white towels, no animals, summery warm.

We drive through the vast deserted resort Ayvalık to the town of Cunda, located on a peninsula, one of the centres of the spa industry. Our pension is located in a small garden next to a battered, partially scaffolded Orthodox Church. It is run by an old woman who, as a child, relocated to Turkey with her parents from their homeland in Crete. Until a few years ago she took care of the abandoned church, showing Greek visitors around, until she was picked up one day in the police car for questioning: she was charged with being a Muslim, Christian 'missionary' woman. Since then, she no longer takes care of the church.

The old woman, barefoot, almost toothless, welcomes guests with many kisses, lovingly boisterous, as if they were relatives who have been long away in a foreign country, returned home. The narrow rooms are of exquisite ugliness. There are two large iron beds in my room. Everywhere else there is leftover stuff, abominations on the walls, an oversized, heavy chair that stands beneath a tiny television which has been mounted too high, making it impossible to watch.

Ülker and I take a bumpy little road down to the beach promenade with empty restaurants on both sides. The desolation of a seaside resort after the season has a Simenon-like charm. Individual waiters stand in front of their fish display cases and point with resignation to the dead fish and their restaurant. We go into one that Ülker knows, and we dine splendidly – lots of green stuff, fried sea bream, Turkish white wine. Ülker tells the story of our landlady, talks about Mustafa Kemal's large resettlement operations in 1923/24. For a millennium and a half Greeks had settled and lived on the Aegean coast (Izmir is the Greek Smyrna). Now they have to go, to be displaced, 'relocated', 'back to the homeland', from Ayvalık, primarily to Crete. (What is homeland for families who for generations, for 'always', have lived in the same country, in the same place?) The evictions were ethnically, linguistically, but also religiously motivated. Greek Orthodox Turks were also said to have been resettled. In return, the Turks were exiled from Greece, had to leave their often considerable possessions, sometimes with little compensation, and build a new life here. They never became 'native': not the Turks here; not the Greeks there.

Next door is a large hall, a cafe, where about fifty men drink tea, play backgammon and look bewildered when we enter the men's shelter and take a seat in a corner. On the way back, we hear music coming from a tavern; we look through the window and the hostess beckons us inside. Three men are playing very loud – violin, drum, a kind of dulcimer, vocals – folk music for two, now four guests, as if we were a hundred. Songs about nightingales and roses. Right in the middle of a different, spirited world. Then, back late through deserted streets on hard, barely passable pavement. Dead silence except for a dog in the distance, who points the way.

Restless night. A crowing cock long before dawn; a nightmare with lots of crouching people I do not know sitting at the tables; a waiting room atmosphere. I want to go. "I must go to Ayvalik"; I miss the tram (no waiting room, after all), and then the train, too.

I'm pulled out of the dream by the loud, throaty voice of a man who is explaining something. Slowly I realise that he is speaking Greek and is probably telling an Orthodox tourist group the history of the church. (It is said to date from the thirteenth century, but looks at first and second glance like nineteenth, eighteenth at most.) Then, women sing droning hymns. From the window I cannot see the group because of the trees in front of it – a pasture, a high mimosa with branches touching the ground. From the side window there is a view of withered mulberry trees, a neglected thicket, corrugated iron shed roofs, and an uninhabited house with empty window openings opposite. Birds – quarreling crows, gulls, sparrows – in the empty window arches of the dilapidated church. On the way down to the promenade I notice the decline everywhere, the crumbling houses, the rubble, all the things thrown away in the gardens and beside the houses. I feel as if everything is standing or laying there abandoned as it was almost a century ago.

In the coffeehouse we meet Önder, the friendly man who will be driving us. He drives us first from Cunda up to a point with a wide panoramic view. We see the many larger and smaller islands, see on the horizon a long wooded mountain range – Lesbos; Mytilene, he says – which lies there like a cloudy dream. Önder knows a great deal; under other conditions, he would certainly have become a teacher. His parents also came over from Crete, and he is apparently still perfectly bilingual. He talks about the green stuff – salads, vegetables, herbs, mostly unknown to me – that the Turkish Cretans brought here with them, about the olive varieties, which is why the most famous oil in Turkey comes from this region and there is such a variety of green. He dismisses the abandoned monastery, the churches, the summer residence of the Metropolitan (who used to be called 'Despot'), which is now a closed military zone. He drives us around to the wide bay, high up to the so-called Devil Kitchen. There, locked in an iron cage, you can see the footprint of Şeitan, of Satan. People throw coins into the hole and make a wish for something. Ülker gives me a coin. There are many low-growing wishing trees – olive, juniper – around it, as I remember them colourfully from Göbekli Tepe. But here they are only hung with white slips of paper, small, snow-dusted Christmas trees, cast out by the poor devil.

The houses of the once wealthy Greeks and Turks are built from so-called garlic stone, a stone that keeps the houses cool in summer and warm in winter. From above, Önder shows us the quarry in a bay. I would like to weigh the stones in my hands and smell them, but they are in the military zone.

The sky has closed and lowered the curtains. It has grown cold and will grow colder. A few luminous spots on the smooth water, where the sun has passed through the thick veil. But the sun itself cannot be seen.

Cunda, Thursday, 13 November 2008

Yesterday the wind only briefly demonstrated its skills; now it is a bright summer day again. We drive through a vast plain to the south, in the direction of Bergama. The fields are almost all harvested: grain, vegetables, sometimes you can still see the white swabs of the last vestiges of cotton. Under low blue nylon strips strawberries are grown for export. On both sides of the road there are large olive plantations. I learn from Önder that in the roots of the trees there is an essence that, if there is enough rain, flows into the branches and forces it to blossom. In dry periods, the essence remains in the root and there are no olives, but the tree does not die. Some of the trees here are supposed to be over two hundred years old. This year it has been too dry; there is only about 30 per cent of the usual harvest.

We are approaching the rather large city of Bergama (80,000 inhabitants; in ancient times it was a major city) and high up on a mountain we see the Acropolis of ancient Pergamon. The car continues up the steep road higher and higher and the complex we have in part driven around, is still monumental.

After a short, tiered footpath, we stand next to the foundations of the oldest and most sacred temple, the one to Athena, a wide empty space that you have to imagine assembled from memory, from the two-storied monumental sanctuary in Berlin, which the king Eumenes had dedicated to the victory bringer Athena. And the Dying Gaul in Rome also belongs here, the first 'realistic' depiction of pain in the twisted legs and contorted face, portrayed as an enemy through the human form! In front of the empty temple area, left of the staircase, far down once stood the overwhelming Great Altar with the battle of the giants and the origin myth of the Attalids, acquired by Berlin in the 1880s, in whose place three huge umbrella pines now cast their shadows over the expanse and the few steps that were not carried away. As monumental as the altar is the landscape in which it stood, and I try to imagine the hundreds of things sacrificed: the cattle, the sheep, the burning aromatic herbs.

Connected to the temple of Athena is the Library, erected again from a series of small pillars. After Alexandria, it was the second largest library of the ancient world, with two hundred thousand books, especially scrolls. Because of competition, Egypt eventually prohibited the export of papyrus, and it is said that a resourceful shepherd here invented parchment from goatskin, named after the city of Pergament, which then made the codex possible, or, as we understand it, 'the book'. Unfortunately, the library was consolidated with the Alexandrian under the Romans. What unknown treasures would probably have been preserved, if they had not had to leave the mountain? All the songs of Sappho, who wrote not far from here? Alkaios? Archilochus?

Immediately after the temple and the library the mountain descends sharply and on this slope was built the steepest amphitheatre in the world, which could hold ten thousand visitors. It is not bordered on either side, and one wonders whether the voices of the actors have not faded away. At the top are the remains of a sound barrier. Therefore the actors must have spoken from the front upwards. From here, the eye is drawn to the middle and lower Acropolis, to the wide valley basin of the Caicos, to the steep mountains opposite with sparse vegetation. There the blue-grey andesite – blue-grey like the kilims woven here to this day – was quarried, from which the previous temple and the theatre were built. Xenophon was here, on the way back with the Greek army, was hospitably received, sacrificed to Zeus and made his last bold foray. (Here the 'Anabasis' breaks off.)

At the highest point of the mountain, the huge Trajaneum stands with is mighty substructures and parts of the re-erected portico. Most striking of all, four pillars across the remains of a frieze, acanthus capitals. In the midday sun the marble gleams in an unearthly, eternal light. Inconceivable that it had once been painted. Despite all its splendor, I am also reminded of the demonstration of power and the sacrilege – the Emperor, who placed his temple above the one for the city's goddess. The temple of Athena must have seemed poor in contrast, a distant memory of a time when the gods were still powerful.

We move on to the rather small palaces of sovereigns, around the Castle Hill; look at the artificial lake deep down below, from which the water was routed up in communicating vessels; go back again through weathered rock, scorched grass, tiny saplings that must have been blown on by the wind, low bushes, which have all persisted against everything that is man-made, and if we go up again and look around us, we are overwhelmed by what the Renaissance painter would have called the Heroic landscape. The silence up here – I want to call it a sublime silence – is only interrupted (or highlighted), after two small tour groups have moved on, by a few bird calls.

Down in the city Ülker buys simit and the three of us find

a seat in front of a teahouse. The men have set up the chairs in rows like seats at the movies and sit in front of the passers-by and the traffic. From a loudspeaker a woman's voice announces the death of a man, listing all of his survivors – there must be a whole village – and the appointed time for the funeral prayer. The old men gaze forward, motionless.

Often, you first read in a guidebook why a ruin is significant. So it was with me and the 'Red Hall', the "most conspicuous building in ancient Pergamum," a temple for the Egyptian gods. Here the extremely high walls were built entirely with red-fired bricks, then covered with marble. The rudiments of massive arches can still be seen, but my imagination is not enough for me to picture a monumental Serapion sanctuary, except to think that it must have been much larger than anything Hadrian, that God, had built, even in the Villa Adriana. Why such a colossus in the province?

Overwhelming, too, the great complex of the Asklepieion, the medicinal and wellness sanctuary, wide expanses between re-erected rows of columns, also from the time of Hadrian. The columns support Doric, Ionic and Corinthian capitals, one next to another, and bear witness to a concurrence. The entire 'history' is on hand; 'evolution' is no longer necessary or is there only in the ingenious engineering. Here, Galen was born. Here, after detours as a doctor for gladiators in Rome, he taught and healed and defined the knowledge of anatomy and humoral pathology for over a millennium. The great silence here has absorbed the past knowledge into itself.

The ride back takes you past pine forests. ("The people here have grown very rich because of the expensive pine nuts.") Sometimes, cowering beside the roadside, there are women coming from the cotton harvest. They have little bundles of brushwood beside them – the result of a day's work scavenging – which they are allowed to take home to use as fuel. When I think of the Arab's big brushwood piles in Harran, I wonder how many days of work it takes to gather together a supply of combustible stuff to last the entire winter. How crooked the backs must become over the years. ("The dream in the crooked back of a farmer.")

Cunda, Friday, 14 November 2008

When I enter my room, my gaze falls on a picture hanging high up between two windows. It reveals a young lady with half-closed, downcast eyes, who has her arms crossed so high behind her head that her virginal bust can be imagined behind her nylon shirt. The shirt opens down into a wool fabric-like pleat over a single leg, which is too long. Left and right of the lady are woolly bulges with the hint of a pinching, caliper-shaped head that may suggest the animalism of science fiction monsters. The picture is bathed in iridescent pink. It is a computer print-out of a painting, probably unsellable. The number 85 is glued to the frame.

Left of the door, above a mirrored dresser with a marble top, hangs a small clock with little feet. Across a clock-face with Roman numerals, the hands indicate quarter to eight.

The clock case is rounded out by a semicircular treasure chest whose small lock could only be opened from a high ladder. No. 83. Beside it on the wall there is a ship's wheel for children, which is covered from the right to left trunnion with a three-master that has been cut in half lengthwise. No number.

On the right wall hangs a hand drum with a bamboo body, mounted at an angle, above an oblong technical instrument which bears the inscriptions Fan and Turbo. Beside it, a leather hash receptacle in the shape of a pear or a devotional image with an empty bottle of Beaujolais. No. 82. (Where is No. 84?)

Between the beds, on a round brass table, there is a huge copper coffee pot that could serve an entire divan, with two wooden trivets in front. Under the two beds there are three pairs of slippers. People have to take their shoes off in the house.

I looked at everything, while I sat at a small round table with a glass top and wrote in my journal, although I tried not to look at the things and to concentrate. What did these stillborn things want from me? I imagined the old Cretan Turkish woman, how she had collected all her life, how she had freed them from their designation as trash and gave them a place where they were allowed to 'be': the superfluous, the overlooked, the useless, the ugly, that which you automatically ignore, which is air to you. When things no longer have life, they should have an afterlife. What is bad taste? The old woman has numbered things in exile and created a catalogue of her treasures. Her aesthetic sense told her to mount the little bamboo drum at an angle, in order to bring the beauty that she feels for it to better advantage. What is beauty?

At noon the sun shines through the window and brings to light the empty sandstone window arches of the dilapidated church, which are surrounded by scaffolding inside and out. Maybe it will even allow Orthodox services once again and contest the ravens' and crows' occupancy. The old streets are by now as familiar as old acquaintances. Everywhere cats, bougainvilleas, tagetes, date palms, friendly people, fish in the many display cases that have not given up, fighting against their earthly destiny.

Cunda, Saturday, 15 November 2008

Around noon we head to the Ida Mountains. Olive plantations. On some trees, the fruit hangs as dense as cherries. Endremit, the centre of the olive riviera on the southern slope of Ida Massif. I imagine how Xenophon with his train of tens of thousands went over the hills and how, in the south, they finally saw the local sea, the Aegean. It must have been closer than today. In Endremit we turn towards the mountains to visit an Alevi village – Tahtakuslar. The Alevis have a hard time as a Muslim minority, though – or because – they are very 'modern' in their thinking. They do not want mosques; they want simple houses of worship, which they do not get. Men and women pray together, celebrate their wedding together. They use candles, which do not exist elsewhere in Islam. They originally derived from Central Asia Turkmen and maintained many shamanic traditions, such as the wishing trees, on whose existence – I know them from Anatolia –their migrations can be traced. They bury their dead with a bed and blanket. Once a year they commemorate with big funerary banquets on the graves.

At the entrance of the village there is a museum. The founder, owner, director and guide all-in-one recounts the history of his people. The Alevis were famous for their wood processing technologies. Here, in the port of Edremit, from the pines and oaks of Ida, they built the fleet which was transported over the land route to the Bosporus and which was used by Mehmed to conquer Constantinople. Here, the guide knows for sure, the Trojan Horse was built, namely from the Nordmann fir (Abies nordmanniana), which we know as the Christmas tree. (I always thought, if only because of the name, that they come from Scandinavia, but they hail from the Caucasus.) Unfortunately, he does not know how and in what period the wooden horse was transported over what is not exactly a short distance to Troy.

In a glass case, he has recreated Ida Massif. As a result, we can, like winged Hermes, survey it completely with its hundreds of rivers and streams. There is Troy; there flows the holy Scamander, from whose summit, usually snowy, Zeus followed the fighting; up there Hephaestus ignited the signal fire to report the fall of Troy, which was further ignited from Lemnos, Euboea, the Messapian Mountains, Kithairon up to Argos, where the watchman, 'on the roof of Agamemnon's palace', waited a year for the signal fire. The old man shows us the place where Paris voiced his fateful judgment: Ayazma. The juxtaposition and interweaving of Greek myth and shamanic presence is self-evident to our guide. In a display case he exhibits the many forms of amulets used against the evil eye (Nazarlik). We could buy some. But it is also enough to grasp your right ear and then knock three times on wood with the same fingers.

Higher up into the mountains, again through olive trees, dense, extensive pine forests, pine, maple, oaks. An elevated truck loaded with pine cones. Every few hundred yards marble fountains, from which we drink the delicious, pure water. Önder has hunted here earlier: there are bears, wolves, wild boar, deer. Now he no longer hunts, out of love for the animals. It is cool, moist – we are now 1,200 metres up – in front of us the mountain ranges and peaks are veiled over. There ahead of us lies the densely forested peak of Ida (1774 metres) where, as we now know, Zeus was enthroned. Schliemann wanted to climb it with his friend Virchow in 1879, but they turned around halfway up because of rainstorms. We look up at the huge round shape which we had dreamed about as grammar school students, from the opposite slope, from the Illiad Hotel. The owner explains that here, or very close to here, he did not know the exact place, Homer wrote the *Iliad*. I ask: are you sure? "Absolutely." How comforting it is to know something for sure.

In the evening we watch *Rembetiko* on Ülker's computer, the film about the expulsion of the Greeks from Smyrna in

1923, the burning houses, the adversity in Piraeus, the recent exclusion from Greek military and police, notwithstanding the conscriptions later in World War II. Humiliation, despair, murders, suicides, a feeling of belonging nowhere-and-never-there. The sad pageantry of the lost and disenfranchised in the rembetiko rhythms of accordion and violin. How little I know, because of my German tunnel vision, of *these* abominations, which continued until the pogrom leading to the destruction of the Greek community in Istanbul in September 1955.

Cunda, Sunday, 16 November 2008

Journal written and typed. In the afternoon, with Ülker to the promenade. Many shops selling jewelry and scarves are open, even without tourists. Summer sightseers from the villages, indulging themselves on the boardwalk with children and ice cream cones. We are sitting in a cafe on the quay in the warm sun and watching the outgoing fishing boats. Suddenly loud music plays from the loudspeaker: the national anthem. People in the cafe rise, the walkers pause in step, the boy bent over the sea washing a bucket straightens himself up, the fisherman lets the rope go. Everything is motionless and silent – a film still. In my many Sundays in Turkey I have never experienced anything like this. Suddenly, I only see 'displaced persons', rootless people, whose history and identity have been taken away through displacement and resettlement. The void has been filled by the prescribed nationalism. ("I am proud to be a Turk.") How these people make me freeze, too.

Izmir, 17 November 2008

By bus to Izmir. The ride through hilly brown landscape, with occasional views of the Aegean Sea, takes three hours, because passengers are picked up on the roadside again and again. The region of Lydia has been inhabited since at least 1000 BCE because of its convenient location, first by the Aeolians, and then by the Ionians, whose philosophy of nature is at the root of Greek thought, which is also our way of thought. Can a landscape spark forms of thought? It was hardly perceived 'as a landscape'. Land was cultivated soil, fields, pasture, timber, wildlife, rain, sun, wind. Nevertheless, I say to myself, in the spirit of all the venerated names before, think of Gyges, of Croesus, of the invention of the coin. Homer was born in the city, which has not been called Smyrna since the twenties. It is, at least, one of his seven or eight birthplaces.

Kilometres long journey to the city of Izmir, home to more than three million; to the left and right of the road a Lego arrangement of houses, termite honeycombs which can only be expanded further inland. From above, from the street, there are no little patches of green between the rabbit hutches to be seen. What is it like in the minds of the people, of the children who live here? Even as we drive into town, the former Greek city seems faceless. Some city. Skyscrapers. Heavy traffic. A boulevard lined with palm trees, at any rate, indicates that the city lies to the south. But the rooms at the Izmir Palas Hotel have balconies overlooking the bay, and the ferry is crossing over it and tooting to the former suburb of Karsiyaka – it was formerly called just Pera, 'Over There' – where once the poor people lived, and today those who are better-off. Cloudy sky.

At noon Renate Elsässer, the director of the Goethe-Institut, picks us up and leads us into a local garden with palm trees and plane trees. A Bougainvillé with yellow flowers. Then the Goethe-Institut, which is housed on the upper floors of a former tobacco warehouse. Everywhere new houses; there is almost nothing left of the old structures, demolished or burned down in the 'resettlement' of the Greeks who founded the city and re-established it and lived here for nearly two thousand years. Apparently, however, it is debatable whether the Turks set their houses on fire, or whether they did it themselves so the Turks could not move into them.

In the evening to a small restaurant with the other director of the Goethe-Institut, Werner Schmidt, and his wife. Greek music. The owner always serves up new delicacies, very strange, including offal stuffed with intestines. (Frau Elsässer assured me they were repeatedly rinsed and washed.) The conversations revolved around the feared Islamisation. Werner Schmidt says that one should not look to the government; they keep a low profile. We had to pay close attention to what is happening on the unofficial stage. School directors who would no longer shake the teachers' hands, because a devout Muslim woman does not shake hands. His Turkish wife, who teaches art at a school, explained that in the past the teachers and students could normally eat in the cafeteria during Ramadan. Today, curtains were drawn and there were only a few people there, who were served brusquely. Nevertheless, in this secular city, the number of women wearing headscarves could be counted on the fingers of one hand, and I have not seen any wearing a full veil.

It is pouring rain, the lights from the opposite shore, from Pera, are no longer visible. After a few steps we are soaked to the skin.

Izmir, Tuesday, 18 November 2008

Early this morning, far out to the university, where I will read from my Anatolian diary and discuss it with the students. A friendly welcome. A student who speaks very good German, who grew up in Germany, says she understood very little, because she lacks the cultural and historical background (which would have actually been her own Turkish background). I say something about the difficulty in many nations, tribes, religious affiliations and their repeated differentiations to be able to speak of 'Turkish' identity. One student, who struggles hard to speak German and does it nevertheless, says that he came from Mardin, was of Kurdish, Armenian and Arabic origin and has problems with the 'Turkish' identity. Dead silence in the hall. Hindsight tells me the young man was very courageous to publicly profess his origins. And in a secular city!

In the Archaeological Museum. The bronze statue of a young athlete in an elegant, jumping run – delicate, fine limbs, while at the same time an ugly sharp-nosed head, but precisely because of that, its 'individualisation' stands out and its proportion in relation to the body rings true. Not to be compared to the stupid shrunken heads on the athletic physique of the classical period. Enchanting, Hellenistic Korai heads, slightly tilted to one side or turned as if to receive a kiss from an approaching god. Androcles, the founder of Ephesus, who I have never seen represented, his head raised high together with the boar. A few early coffins made of limestone – on their sides geometric patterns, meanders; in orbit above, also engraved in black, animal images, lions, griffins, and sphinxes. This type of coffin is also new to me. The famous relief statues of Poseidon and Demeter are nowhere to be seen.

From the museum down the mountain – Pagos, where Alexander dreamed (how many times?) of rebuilding Smyrna – to the bazaar. Here below the river Meles must have flowed. It is mentioned in Homer, which is why Smyrna claims to be the birthplace of the poet. The bazaar is spread out over a wide area, with the usual streets organised according to crafts or goods. In front of the stores, in the middle of the road, young men stand and hold up jeans which they turn in all directions to exhibit the good workmanship. Even on the narrow path there are traders with hot chestnuts, boiled corn on the cob, and mussels with lemon. One is carrying a box of transparent plastic gloves in front of him; one is carrying a three-legged table on his head, which contains a tray with freshly baked simit. Ülker points out a schmalzkringel in the back of a baker's window, which in translation is called 'sweet':

in Istanbul such a donut would always be offered in front of the brothels. An admission ticket. I admire the hurrying boys with tea trays, who skillfully dodge and evade every possible blow from the crowd, almost dancing. In between the chaos there are three mosques, including the famous Hisar Mosque dating from the sixteenth century, with a large central dome. I will not go inside because it is already dusk, and I would not be able to see the uniform, diffused light. In the old caravanserai dating from the eighteenth century, one of the rare Ottoman structures in the predominantly Greek city, Kizlavagasi, we drink tea.

I notice the many restored, one-story houses, some with cast iron railings and balconies. They are the former homes of the Greeks. The Turks built with wood. A simpler, immediately recognisable style, with tasteful, restrained colours: ocher, brown, and grey.

After many questions we find the synagogue – Ets Hayin Synagogue, the Tree of Life Synagogue. A two-story building; on the first floor six straight, limestone façade windows; above them, six with round arches. Because the plaster has crumbled away in many places, we can see that the bottom floor once had round windows. The emerging wall, composed of stones of various sizes, indiscriminately cobbled together from whatever could be found: field stones, larger scraps, no red brick anywhere.

A merchant has been watching us as we stand there, and tells us that there were 1,300 Jews in Izmir; sometimes they held their worship services and then there were always six policemen present. Was there anti-Semitism in Izmir? "No, no. It was because of the attack on a synagogue in Istanbul." Then he leads us to the other synagogues nearby: Hevra, Algaze, Sinyora Giveret, Salom, Bet-il-El. It is noteworthy that 'synagogue' is written in Turkish sometimes, and sometimes French (or English), and that not a single Hebrew letter is used. Except for the first and the last synagogue, everything looks unused and deserted.

We climb up to the archaeological site Agora: a huge square with columns erected on two sides. Below the square we can see a low-lying street of merchants with arcade arches. Above, the great Poseidon and Demeter relief which I was not able to see this afternoon, was found. The wide area is fenced off and martially barred. Ülker suggests that we climb over the guard railing. I'm not quite sure. We go a little further up and find an open entrance. In front there are guards with dogs, who will not allow us to take even one step onto the grounds. When we descend again to the fence, we see one of the dogs roaming the area. When he sees us, he barks at us angrily, even though he had seemed peaceful a moment ago. Maybe we would have been subjected to his fangs if we had climbed over.

We walk towards the sea and it starts to rain, harder and harder, a cloudburst, as if all the rain prayed for but withheld by Allah during the last year would be dumped over us.

In a matter of seconds, soaked to the skin for the second time in this city, we rescue ourselves in a taxi.

Cunda, Thursday, 20 November 2008

Yesterday Renate Elsässer and a friend picked us up at the hotel to drive south to Ephesus. We rode along the bay where there were many container ships waiting to dock in the port of Izmir. A day in the waiting queue will cost ten thousand dollars. Along the bay, on the left, are the same apartment houses everywhere with the same paned balconies, tightly packed. Again and again another hill is covered with buildings from top to bottom. Within a single summer, a whole hill is fully cluttered. The city of Izmir stretches out on all sides, the modern form of lava from a volcano that suffocates everything grown. Once upon a time it was the acclaimed pearl of the Aegean.

We take a turnoff to Teos and after a few minutes we are in another world: low, whitewashed houses, tangerine plantations, a row of women assigned to check the fruit in the boxes. Then a view, first of a small bay, then a larger one. Teos was once the city with the biggest Dionysos sanctuary of ancient times. By now it is raining so hard that it is not easy to visualise the famed bucolic aura. By foot through the mud and there in the rain are fragments of beams with egg-and-dart motifs, snails, meanders, remnants of acanthus capitals. Perhaps among them, as they stood, sat Anacreon, who here in Teos loved and caroused and wrote poetry. Perhaps he sang as he leaned against one of the olive trees that are so thick here that they may have survived for centuries.

In this weather, would Anacreon have fabricated in his poetry the sun, which he tasted in the wine and 'recollected in tranquility'? A farmer trots by on his donkey, saluting, from a high basket at the edge protrudes a folded stroller.

Quite soaked through, we continue our journey along the coast, high up, steeply down, left and right pinewood, umbrella pine, short juniper, thyme, rosemary, under a woolly canvas of clouds in various shades of grey which is riddled with meagre spots of blue. At a height to the left side of a small meander, a swamp with cows and storks, there is a clear view of the very large island of Samos in the distance.

We turn inland and approach Ephesus, which was once a port city on the sea. But the river Kaystros, with its swans and cranes, is filled with sand. Even from a distance you can see the theatre, which provided space for twenty-four thousand spectators. Paul preached here. In front of a full house? It is said that Luke and John are buried in the town. Did they also die here? In this city a council argued over the question of whether Mary was the mother of Jesus's physical body only or also of His divine nature.

We climb from the bottom to the top of the monumental, magnificent city, once burned down by Herostratus, then rebuilt by Lysimachus, and then the capital of the Roman province of Asia. I try to imagine everything Hellenistic and Roman which has been excavated and the cluster of Asian, and American, Italian and German visitors, and I picture Heraclitus in the empty landscape, but among the same vegetation that exists today ("How can one hide from that which never sets?") as he devised his cryptic proverbs: "War (polemos) is the father of all things." (With whom had he argued? Or had he actually had in mind the war which destroyed his town, founded by Androklos?) The famous 'Panta Rhei', there is nothing permanent but change. Or: "Into the same river we step and yet we do not step": here, this here – this stone, this shrub – is the present and is yet again not; is what has been or the unchanging. Or: "The name of the bow (biós) is life (bíos), but its work is death." That is an even shorter image than Beckett's "They give birth astride of a grave".

Can a person, among the crowds of tourists, in front of the monuments described a hundred times, notice anything? (Heraclitus also said, "Nature – physis – loves to hide itself".) A roly-poly American in front of the Temple of Hadrian is talking on his cell phone: "Right now we are at the place where Mary came to death." (Why didn't he say 'died'? Or does he consider her a martyr? And the House of the Virgin is far away, high up in the forests. The fat guy would have barely managed to make it up there.) Two women come out of the Library of Celsus and the one says to the other: "If you've seen one library you've seen them all." (This is reminiscent of the statement about the Californian redwood trees Ronald Reagan wanted to have cut down.) Most people here – in their physicality, their gait, their fluorescent-coloured parade, their faces, their commentaries – are extras in a Fellini film.

But there is the keystone on the pediment of Hadrian's Temple: the goddess Tyche with flowing hair, the crown on her head depicting the walls of the city, the abundance of gifts underneath – an almost anachronistic, mannerist oriented reference in memory of a time when Tyche protected the city. There are two tapered statues of Hercules at the gate named after him. There is the imprint of a woman's foot as a guidepost to the brothel. There is one of the four allegories on the façade of the Celsus Library, lips slightly parted. Is it Ennoia? Is it Episteme? I forgot to write it down. Incidentally, it is quite ingenious that the library (twelve thousand scrolls) is actually a tomb.

Against the ever stronger downpours we take refuge at the lower entrance to the city, under the tarpaulin roofs of the souvenir merchants: in addition to the 'genuine fake watches' (as advertised), Artemis statues in every size and weight. It is understandable that the silversmith Demetrius started a rebellion against the preacher Paul and that the slogan 'Great is Diana (Artemis) of Ephesus' rang out for hours. It was not all about the defense of the ancient gods against the pronouncement of the new one. It was about the inability to make a visual representation, and therefore the inability to sell this particular one. It was the revolt of the souvenir traders who feared for their business, which they carry on successfully down to the present day.

And in the museum at the nearby Seldcruk you can see the statue of Artemis, about three metres high, festooned with dozens of bull testicles, an adorable, awe-inspiring ('awful') image of fertility and potency compared to the invisible God.

We climb up the steep road through the pretty Ottoman town to the Isa Bey Mosque. Along the way, recurring signs point the way to a 'Homeros Pension' with a "family atmosphere". In front of the mosque we meet a souvenir trader who is also the imam. He comes up to us and tells the story of the mosque, built in 1375, which is said to hold three thousand people. High granite columns, from Aswan he says (but excavated in Ephesus), with Corinthian and Ottoman capitals. Ülker asks him if he, like many here in the last few days, has also prayed for rain. (That the prayers were successful, we have felt on our own bodies the last two days.) "Yes," he says, "but Allah also gives, even if we do not pray. He is so great, so kind, and so compassionate. He gives to us from His fullness", and his eyes fill with tears. "There is only one God", he continues, "the God of the Jews, the Christian God, our God; there is only one, and he gives to us from His fullness." (Ülker says it is a memorised recitation, used to engage various customers.) What is the difference between this offering to God and the heavy sacks of bull testicles hanging on Artemis?

Cunda, Friday, 21 November 2008

Wrote all day yesterday and this morning transcribed it with Ülker's help and sent it along with photographs to Istanbul. Insh'Allah.

In the afternoon, over to Ayvalık in the Dolmusch. We sat on the shore with sandwiches, in front of a stage prop sea, islands, graduated grey-blue stratus layers, light wind, the water foaming, and seagulls, their gliding flight changing constantly because of the thermal gradients.

In the small seaside nest we are looking for surviving Christian churches. No one knows anything about them, but we are referred to someone in a German-run boarding house. We find her after much questioning: Annette, who has lived here for over twenty years. Ayvaltk was purely a Greek village; you can see it even in the stone houses. Since 1923 there have only been Turks, without history and tradition, who assert a particularly 'persuasive' nationalism. (Here, the first shot was fired against the Greeks who were given a mandate to rule after the First World War.) There are no longer Christian churches; the exercise of the Christian faith is prohibited, as well as, at least in earlier times, the use of the Greek language. You had to pay a penalty if a Greek word passed your lips if, for example, you did not know the Turkish one. (As we know similarly of the Kurds, the Armenians, and the Arabs.) The people of Ayvahk live in what is a prime example of what Benedict Anderson has described as an 'imagined community'. Did she, Annette, have friends here after all these years? Well, yes, a few, further away, although Turks lived in her boarding house, not tourists; but to the neighbours she has always been the mistrusted foreigner. Indeed she was not a willing Christian woman professed of the Christian faith, but the fact alone that she has no affiliation with Islam made her suspect of being an 'infidel'. And naturally she had not become a nationalist. How could she? My God, it is not about minorities and their quite understandable, at least debatable, aspirations of autonomy here – or at least acceptance. Here there is 'only' a minimum of tolerance towards 'the other'. How little we know about this country, which seems to be predestined by its many peoples, cultures, traditions, religions, to be 'European'. That would work, I think, for the Westerners, for all of them, except for the nationalists.

In the evening a visit to see one of Claudia's friends, an old lady, a Circassian, in an elevated house with a beautiful garden and views over the bay. She was born in Kars; her parents came down from the Caucasus in 1917. "We Circassians have no problems. We have mixed marriages; we are Turks; our language is dying out in the younger generation. Well, too bad", and her wise eyes confirm it without resignation: that's how it is. On the taxi ride to the old, wonderful, singing, German-speaking lady – she had lived a few years in Munich – the sun was already going down. Red over Lesbos, and the squadron of clouds above it were illuminated in a delicate pink. Then an aggressive wind blew once more into Cunda from the bay. The fishing boats crashed into the quay wall and the canvas covers on the beach cafes jerked clattering at their moorings. Now, about midnight, the windows rattle and the shutters bang; the wind penetrates through the cracks, tilting the painting of the pink lady between the beds in my room at a crooked angle. The branches of the willow outside the window lash the earth.

Cunda, Saturday, 22 November 2008
Bad night. Either Aeolus has unleashed all his winds at once, or they have been reciting their allegiance to him. The old

house crashes and rumbles in all its joints, and the four shutters thunder from time to time. In the morning, the wind still has the same force. All the same, we want to drive from Önder to Troy. Our landlady says she will pray for us.

We drive up the coast to the churning sea. It is the rare south wind, the Greek Nothio, which is to be feared: a winter wind. With the views down to the sea I imagine the fleets of the Achaeans, as they made their way along here (in the Archaic period there was almost exclusively coastal navigation), as they crashed against the rocks during a storm and lost men and ships. Above us the sea of clouds, an almost closed blanket, the horizon indistinguishable from the water. Past the extensive Ida Mountains, the heavens of Zeus are also covered with a cloud haze. On the fields we can see still the red dots of the low tomatoes; the beans, peas, and peppers have been harvested. Most hills are, for many kilometres, planted from bottom to top with olive trees. We come into Troas. Here, the abundant holm oaks catch the eye. Then to Troy.

The compound, not very large, has good signage. You read, 'East Gate', 'Battlements', 'Megaron houses', and see the paved ramp that leads up to the castle. Many a smooth wall of irregular bricks, joined without mortar, makes you wonder about the art of masons before the Iron Age. But basically there is nothing for the untrained eye 'to see'; the place is 'created' by what we bring with us in our minds: Gustav Schwab's legends about classical antiquity from childhood, the *Iliad* from a bit later. The wonderful Helios-relief in Berlin, with the four rearing steeds from the Temple of Athena, excavated by Schliemann. And the excavation stories, told by Schliemann and Dörpfeld, are more vivid in the mind than what is in front of our eyes. But today Ilion has a special aura for us: we were right in the thick of a battle of the winds. They were so violent that we sometimes lost balance and we had to shout in order to hear each other. The angry, snorting, hissing, roaring, panting, howling wind struck at the fig trees, tamarisks, and oak trees that they threatened to break. We had to 'defend' ourselves: dodge, turn, reverse, crouch, rise, feint, and there was a new blow to parry from continually changing directions. During lulls in the fighting we looked like generals on the plain where the Greek armies stood and the ships lay, a little further away than the distance of an arrow shot, although God could sometimes guide the shot further. Beyond the armies, also within sight of the Dardanelles, the Hellespont.

Opposite the small Roman theatre there is something to learn: on a multi-branched, fat old holm oak hangs a sign: 'Quercus Troiana', and on it there are five references to oaks from Homer, like these: "nor such again the crying voice of the wind in the deep-haired oaks, when it roars highest in its fury against them" (Il.14.398) – but by who? Achilles, Ajax, Hector? (I see later: "as now the noise of Achaians and Trojans in voice of terror rose as they drove against one another...")

On the return journey the enraged Poseidon is truly in his element and lets the Tritons and Nereids whip up the sea so tidal waves flood the streets. The storm grows stronger. Six fishing boats have already sunk here in the bay. The town, including our house, is without electricity. The landlady's son runs to the village to get candles. The shutters in my room are barred shut, since the latches are broken. Now, in the evening, the rain god has also opened the floodgates.

Cunda, Sunday, 23 November 2008

Poseidon has ordered that his horses be returned again and placed in the stables. "Dull and empty the sea."

We drive up once again to Alevitendorf, towards the snow-capped peak of Ida. The friendly caretaker from the other day told us that they, the Alevis, at least the ones in these parts, had made a compromise: they had taken from Islam what appeared useful to them, and had modernised their ancestral ancient shamanism. In former times you had had to drink the blood of thirty horses at a funeral; now you can take it instead from a single ram. He talks about the feasts for the dead, held on the graves, to which the neighbours brought along baked bread. The cemetery is laid out in a pine forest overlooking the wide bay. Here the many whitewashed brick fireplaces immediately catch the eye, then the tall clay pots on each grave for water, wine, or oil. The graves must be left at rest a year before they are finished with marble. At the head and foot of the fresh graves there are low wooden columns in an implied human form, each wrapped with many glittering silks as a symbol of the wish given to the dead to take with them in their transition into the new world of eternal spring. Death as a rejoicing, constantly renewed through a feast of art.

We drive even higher up Mount Ida, looking for Ayazma, the site of the judgement of Paris. Along the way peach plantations, vineyards in the cold altitude, a maple forest in brown autumn leaves. Our hunter Önder shows us partridges, a low-flying hawk, a falcon. Then, still higher, cherry and, unmistakably, apple after apple trees: we must be on target. The place is a narrow gorge, in its considerable depth a hurried brook flows into the valley. To the right, pines – as tall as a ship's mast, straight up sometimes – on the other side holm oak forests, in between uncommon meadows with a little hut. By foot further into the canyon, we walk about two kilometres, streams and creeks from everywhere, at one point three flowing torrents together, one of which should flow with hot water in the summer. ("The sick Aphrodite bathed," the guard in Alevitendorf knew, "in the hot water." But he had forgotten why she was sick.) All steeply downhill, precipitous, so you wonder where the shepherd Paris could find a grazing area for his sheep. The road widened at one point so two cars could pass one another, and there was also a metal sign here, with words to the effect of: Here the exiled prince Paris decided the dispute between the three goddesses, which Zeus was too diplomatic to settle. Here bribery worked for the first time: Hera promised him dominion over Asia and Europe; Athena promised to make him a great hero, Aphrodite, etc. Why the imagination selected this modest little pastoral spot, hardly a suitable location for the three goddesses' big performance, remains a mystery. The abundance of water, certainly, the lush vegetation in comparison to the rest of Ida, the agreeable coolness in the summer heat.

But the canyon, the narrowness, the vertical, steeply sloping, bleak mountain above? It's rather the place for Priam's son, abandoned, to commit his destruction. As is so often the case, different strands of tradition seem to be interwoven; the poets and painters did not take any interest in something as trivial as the reference to local conditions. But why, conversely, are there people with the strange desire to know for themselves, through myth and poetry, not to mention religious tradition, 'how it really was'? Is it the residue of an atavistic aspiration to be able to touch on a secret that is determined in the aura of a stone, a tree, a trickling brook, and might reveal itself?

A few yellow and brown leaves on the trees in the wind, that desperately want to break away from their prescribed attachment. A trembling dog. He will die soon, Ülker says.

Cunda, Monday, 24 November 2008

Along the now-familiar road to Endremit, the snowy peaks of Ida as a backdrop, then a turn-off down to the bay, towards Assos. In the olive tree plantations, where there are still a few ancient trees, women with large plastic buckets collect the olives shaken off by the wind over the last few days. Lesbos comes into view – the summit looks like a female breast with an erect nipple (a horrible word for something that represents so much tender desire). Assos, the now famous little town, is built on a volcanic hill and as a result the preserved or restored walls – Cyclopean walls – have been heavily fortified. Between the walls there are large flocks of sheep, which are rarely seen in the area. Abundant greenery, growing exuberantly, mostly with lancet-shaped, smooth or furry leaves, among the labyrinthine white veined spurge with small thorns. Massive sarcophagi, about three feet long, are scattered in among the greenery, lids beside them, probably taken by grave robbers. Pliny tells us of a special stone in the area of Assos that allows the corpses to decompose more quickly than other stones. Hence the name sarcophagus – 'Flesh eating'. We drive up the steep road and stop in front of a cafe, to eat a snack and afterwards to drink a coffee, which is mixed with mastic, and Önder says that the coveted, therefore expensive mastic is smuggled from the Greek islands and transferred at sea from fishing boat to fishing boat. By foot further up the steep bumpy path to the summit, past a low, unplastered stone cottage, which looks Greek. (Assos was founded by Lesbians.) On both sides, long rows of empty tables with useless awnings above them. At one table a woman sits and hopes to sell us her colourful towels and hand-knitted baby slippers. An old man squats on the ground in front of a house and arranges wood and kindling pieces lengthwise. A couple of mopeds and cars, an old tractor. Sporadic old people who walk very slowly and look lost to us.

The Temple of Athena, built in the fifth century BCE, stands at the top of the summit, from where the view crosses far over the Aegean Sea, to the Greek islands, Lesbos, and Mytilene, directly opposite. Five pillars have been re-erected, the capitals in Doric order. There are a few tambours from the columns scattered around, a few of the column parts – crown, capital, plinth for the upper entablature – are upended. All of this has a massive simplicity, if one can say so, a serene force of in-this-and-not-in-any-other-way. There is no chisel mark too much or too little. There is no scrollwork winding itself around, there is nothing playfully Corinthian. There is only the imperturbable calm of a being, like an old tree. There is only the immense silence, illuminated by a cold, midpoint sun on Lesbos, made audible by distant goat bells. I imagine Sappho sitting on the opposite shore, pondering the boat in which a young man – 'godlike' – leads one of her favourite girls away to the wedding. Maybe she looks on the bright limestone of the Temple of Athena and asks: "Why?" Could her gazes still be sensed at the star? The ancients understood the gaze as something material – the line of sight consisted of tiny particles that cling to what they have seen, but also pierce a glimpsed eye, could with its barbs arrest other hearts and kindle love – completely 'concrete', completely physical – like a woodpile. Perhaps her gaze clung to the stones, which were sealed for centuries under the earth?

Two mirage-hunters break the spell. On the descent an old man sells us a bouquet of thyme. It is mostly thyme that grows on the meadows, giving the local sheep their particular flavour, he says. The late sun casts bright spots on the smooth sea. Our shadow runs ahead of us.

We drive down to the sea and climb up the steps of the theatre. At one point, the benches materialise from top to bottom like the steps of Titans. Paul preached here on his last journey. Would anyone want to listen to him while looking at the sea and across to Lesbos?

Cunda, Wednesday, 26 November 2008

We set out at 7 o'clock in the morning for Tenedos to reach the ferry by 10:00. There should still be a few old Greek families left in Turkey who might be willing to talk about their lives. But when we arrive at the harbour and have paid for the crossing, the sea is restless, and that means that the ferry may not be able to make the return journey in the evening, that we must stay overnight, and it was not certain whether it would be able to sail the next morning. It is known that Poseidon, especially in the vicinity of Troy, cannot be trusted. He left his steeds, which hurried like the wind, in a grotto between Tenedos and the larger island of Imvros for the moment, where he could most advantageously help the Achaeans in their struggle against the ships that wanted to destroy the Trojans. So we do not take the boat over to Tenedos, which in any case was destroyed by Achilles, and go instead to Troas, the country-side around Troy, to the old city of Alexandria Troas, which I wanted to see anyway.

The city centre is still located by the sea, as once was Troy, and that gives a better idea of how the Achaeans moored the ships here. Both cities were competing with their ports: it is said that Caesar wished to have built the capital of his empire here, not in Troy. It is said that here, not in Troy, Constantine had the same plan for the centre between Asia and Europe and had already started to build before he opted for Byzantium; here Paul had a dream that told him to move on to Macedonia to Christianise Eurasia.

The kind caretaker explained: Alexandria Troas was not an evolved city, but a planned one. Sixty thousand people had lived here. The hammam – we could still see the huge entrance gate – is the biggest among the ancient ruins in Asia Minor. We walk with him between holm oaks across the extensive grounds with a view of the sea, through harvested cornfields with stony soil where children are looking for coins after the rain. That was this; that was that. An archaeologist from Münster, Elmar Schwertheim, dug here, but a lot had not yet been excavated. The East Gate, pieces of the fortress wall, a castle – or perhaps a temple complex – people did not agree. This inscription here states that the sanctuary of Apollo should be governed from here. The few precious artefacts – a headless eagle – had been taken away to museums, and he shows them to us on his digital camera. The Olympic Games were also held here. The rules are known from local discoveries; here is the stadium. We walk over grass, nettles, chamomile, spurge, a plant growing everywhere in tufts that has daffodil-like leaves – asphodel, the Flower of Hades? – but the woody spadices do not look right. They are called Kirislik, but I cannot find it in my dictionary. Olive trees, holm oaks, junipers, and in between broken granite columns. How nice it is that most do not 'decay', but rest under the protective soil in a nameless forsakenness. The theatre, in which Paul preached, has been reclaimed by nature. Beautiful. From the sea a sharp wind is steadily blowing upward and, if they say of Troy that the wind brought the city its wealth, then it must have also been true for Alexandria Troas, with its many covered market streets.

The terrain is so vast that we travel there by car, to the hammam, with the gate and its granite aqueducts, to the necropolis hills, still peaceful. A grave has been forced open by a robber, but no one knows what he found beneath it. The entire hill, of considerable extent, (how many dead are buried there?) belonged to a goatherd – we see him later with his flock – but he could not do anything with it; building was not allowed here. He would only get some money when the excavations began. Ibrahim, the guard, talks about the flesh eating stones, which are also in this area. They devour everything: flesh, hair, bones; only the teeth remained. The stone contained sulfuric acid, but that had become known only recently. Ibrahim talks about Apollo, the man they call the Mice Man here because his arrows had turned into mice in order to bring the plague to the Trojans. He talks about Aristotle, who had lived not far from here for three years, in Assos, and found his wife there. He also talks about himself and his ten years as a soldier in Southeast Anatolia, on the Syrian border: constant quarrels with the minorities, nightly raids by PKK members, the dead on both sides, and often you did not even know who had made a pact with whom or who was who. "But here in Troas, here is paradise." He talks and talks, the river of words momentarily coming to a halt at times, and Ülker has trouble translating for me.

In a small village we stand at the hot mineral springs, which has twenty small bath houses that are still used. The water is so hot that I pull my hand away quickly. Paul submerged a dead man in the water here and brought him back to life. Nearby a cool spring gushes – it prevents eye diseases, so we splash our faces. And we drive even higher into the mountains, to a large granite quarry. Here is a place which looks as if the workers had just left at closing time. Six gigantic, hewn and polished columns of equal length – I guess twenty metres – and of equal diameter – I guess a half metre – grey-brown, lying on the ground fifteen hundred years or more and waiting for transport to Rome or Byzantium. Ibrahim wants to go on and on, and we have not yet encountered the old city of Neandros. What is that there? A wall – but we can no longer follow him, and leave him in his paradise.

Helmuth von Moltke visited Alexandria Troas on his fact-finding trip to Turkey and lamented its decline. But what of this city, this place, would have remained if it had continued to exist to the present day? Nothing.

Cunda, Friday, 28 November 2008
Yesterday Moni came from Frankfurt for two days. She does not find the house as horrible as I do (I suppose it is no longer true), kindly points out the simply carved, parallel wooden

stairs that lead to the second floor, the tidy patchwork of carpets laid out everywhere that, if you look at them only fleetingly, could be kilims. (The old woman probably had to sell the real ones, if she ever owned any.) Moni also quickly finds out that the numbers on the objects, which I considered ennobled trash, come from an antique dealer. So we live in a shop that no one enters but us. (Anything that is more than 5 or 10 years old seems to be considered antique here. So time goes by quickly here; in the ruined houses all around us, on the other hand, it stopped at some point.)

Lunch on the sunny quay in the warm November sun. A fishing boat slowly approaches. Immediately, cats come scurrying from everywhere, a dozen, two dozen, three. They pause at the quay wall, their necks stretched out, their bodies taut, silent, and motionless. In some cases they shift their weight from one front foot to the other. Silent goddesses who wait for their due sacrifice.

Today in Bergama. Through Moni's eye, a photographer's, I notice things that I had not seen the first time. On the entablature of the Temple of Trajan, the series of small, apotropaic Medusa's heads, which she zooms the lens in on. Not the archaic form of the protruded tongue; just a horrified, slightly opened mouth, empty eye sockets, the wild lion's mane, and under the head two ionic coils, like abstract breasts – no longer symbols of horror, but tamed in the tiny decorative ornament. In the face of the giant fluted columns with their massive Corinthian capitals, they barely attract attention.

We roam through the countryside and ask ourselves which of the ruined temples may have held the Throne of Satan, which is mentioned in the book of Revelation, then we follow a sign down to the Mosaic Museum. The steep trail leads past the base of the great altar, which has been removed, past the grave of Carl Humann, the excavator of Pergamon, leads through the upper Agora pass and then branches out, so we ascend again and want to give up again. When I look up by chance, I see two gesticulating men at the stairs to the car park, who apparently followed our descent and assume where we want to go. They draw the direction and changes in directions several times in the air with their hands, and so we climb down again. Everything on the walls appearing in the far distance turns out to be the remains of something, but by scrabbling around in the sand there we discover nothing Mosaic-like.

We ascend again and now, through the binoculars, I see how high above us the men are still standing, shaking their heads and pointing their hands even further down. So, a third time. Finally, after half an hour, we are facing a newly built hall. A pair of guards who sit smoking in a cage look at us in wonder, because apparently strangers do not find their way here. The large-scale mosaics hardly compensate for the long march. Conventional plant and animal representations, gods' heads. But the guidebook provides details of a once local mosaic, now in Berlin. It is signed, as mosaics often are: lying there on the mosaic as if casually tossed off is a musivic 'slip of parchment', *Hephaistion epoiei*, pasted to the background

at three corners with red wax, the fourth corner has acciden-
tally detached from the base and rolled up – a *trompe l'oeil*! A
memento of sudden dissolution, of inevitable decay, but in a
work intended to last for generations. – In the photographs
in the guidebook the border of the mosaic is still pictured:
'reciprocal' combs, that is, combs whose teeth are interwoven alternately black and white, 'positive' and 'negative', thus,
they spring into view between the foreground and the surface
beneath and thereby creating the illusion of something floating. In addition, a central Anatolian kilim from the nineteenth
century is reproduced in the book – with the same motive.
There are nearly two thousand years between the mosaic and
the kelim. An example of the continuity of forms through
the centuries, seamlessly changing peoples and cultures and
religions as durable as the plants under our shoes. Were they
merely ornamental or did they have an apotropaic function
– even in the knitted fabric of the 'unhistorical' peasants of
Anatolia?

Down to the Asklepieion. We trot a good kilometre along
the renovated, deserted Via Sacra. At the end, one of the four
or five sacred springs, the water bubbling from a metal pipe.
The layout of the bathhouses, healing dormitories, latrines.
(Here, it is said, stood a statue of the god Donacacato, who
was responsible for the digestive tract.) It was only when we
leave the tidy archaeological district and walk up a grass hill
that something of the aura of the place arises in the afternoon
silence. Thistles, thorns, ancient olive trees left standing as if by

chance, cypresses, scattered sheep. Stones that have not been turned over and over. Lizards, salamanders, which have eternal life. Trickling water that is only there to listen to. The buzz of cicadas. Butterflies, those silent soul-birds, fluttering, colourful omens against the sky, and there in the lost dawn on the short grass we are aware that Asklepios is sending us a dream, to explain to us that this ancient knowledge is missing.

Istanbul, Sunday, 30 November 2008

Yesterday farewell to our Charikleia, sobbing in pain, kissing us many times. In Ayvalik, we buy a 10-litre canister of oil ('The best oil in all of Turkey'), then by car through dreary country to Izmir. From there to here.

This morning the great cistern, Yerebatan. It is a vast subterranean, columned hall, like a Romanesque crypt, but between the columns, instead of sarcophagi, there is water. It was the reservoir holding the water supply for the nearby Topkapi Palace. Spectral artificial light, haze, humidity. We cross the water over long, slippery bridges. Under a column at the end there is a giant head of Medusa on the crown. Presumably, the column was erected upside down in order to banish the terrors, in the way the reversed read or spoken words in magic impart power over the spirits. According to legend, King Solomon built the vault as a prison for the rebellious jinn. Now – we see it – people touch the mouth and chin of the Medusa and hope for luck.

In the Hagia Sophia, through the Emperor's Gate and into the pillarless, gigantic room, where the 'normal' believers are not admitted. "The surprising thing is the great openness of the space, 8,000 square feet, spanned by a single vault. Our Christian cathedrals are like a forest with slender stems and broad leaf crowns; these domes are the firmament itself imitated." (Moltke). Under the legendary dome, the scope of which you can pace off by means of marks on the floor. Two half-domes support the high dome, but this has not been widely known. Thus, over the centuries, the ever-expanding support structures outside. In the crown of the dome there was once a mosaic of the Christ Pantocrator; now the circle has been painted over. At the foot of the giant dome hang glaring white tondi with the holy name. (Kemal Pasha had them removed when he wanted to make the mosque a museum, but because of their size they would not fit through the Imperial Gate and they were hung up again.) The mihrab was installed in the former altar area, shifted from its axis to the right, to align it to Mecca (rather than Jerusalem). But this intervention must have been somewhat distorted to the array of hundreds of Moslem worshipers, because "the venerable millennial Matron", as Moltke called the Hagia Sophia, "turns away from the tomb of the Prophet and looks east, into the face of the rising sun, south towards Ephesus, Antioch, Alexandria, Corinth and the grave of the Redeemer, to the west, which she left, and to the north, from which she awaits liberation."

A ramp up to the broad, columned entrance for the ordinary believers – and for synod assemblies – was designated. On the walls mosaics of emperors and empresses have been uncovered. The Tomb of the Doge Enrico Dandolo, the blind nonagenarian who rerouted the Fourth Crusade to Constantinople in 1204, conquered the city, ravaged and raided for three days, brought Venice large territorial gains, established the Latin Empire and died here.

A deesis – Christ triumphant with hands held in benediction – from the twelfth or thirteenth century, when the Man of Sorrows had already replaced the old iconography in the West. When viewed from above what you notice below, in front of the altar, is a circular slab of marble: the place where the Emperor was crowned. It is called the omphalos – the centre of the world. But because of the few small windows the entire, mammoth room, surveyed from the gallery, presents itself in mystical semi-darkness. When it was still obscured in a cloud of incense smoke, perhaps not far away the reminder of the Pythia was rendered gigantic, superhuman.

After so much oppression, severity, and minuteness of human life, it was a relief to walk into Sinan's Sokollu Camii. (Sokollu was a vizier under Suleiman.) Everywhere brightness, light up in the farthest corner, even an exhilaration when faced with the lack of mystery in what is not hidden, revealed in front of you. On the mihrab there are two small posts that could have been turned by hand and so indicated that the static was in order. But now only one can be turned! So there is indeed a mystery – it is that of Sinan's ingenious art. The vaulted ornamentation (muqarnas) is carved of limestone: over the lintels, for capitals, in borders, repeated in different sizes inside and out, like a single recurring motif – sometimes forte, sometimes piano – in a composition.

In the afternoon we sit in front of the Süleymaniye, drinking Turkish coffee and looking up at the southern front of this monumental building, which is said to excel Solomon's Temple and the Church of Constantine and Justinian in its magnitude. (Incidentally, 'Suleyman' is the Arabic form of "Solomon".) Uniform grey marble from the Marmara Sea. The supporting ramps are attached to the outside, but fit, unlike the Hagia Sophia, harmoniously into the whole, while inside, as Ülker describes, they are so integrated that you are completely unaware of the transition from the circle of the dome to the square of the space. Unfortunately, the entire interior is still surrounded by scaffolding and cannot be entered. We walk around the large mosque area – through the lattice your attention is drawn right to the very austere façade – and outside you see the small mausoleum which Sinan designed for himself. What humility, to have a resting place for yourself outside – as a 'signature' under his work – and not in the vast mausoleum of the Sultan's family, which Süleyman had offered to him as the highest distinction. From the street you can see through the lattice to a simple marble sarcophagus with a turban, and above it a small canopy with the stalactite motif at the four corners. Schlichter's can hardly be any larger. The grave stands at a sharply angled street corner. In front of it Sinan had a fountain put in place, still bubbling, his kindness beyond death.

In the evening at Claudia Hahn-Raabe's, who has invited two young authors and a Turkish-Jewish poet, Ronnie Markulis. The three play around with their 'Turkish' identity. Each of them says something mischievous to the other, which is acknowledged with loud laughter by the rest. Ronnie says to Arrnenierin: "Your language is the most horrible there is: 'ward' for *rose*. Horrible. All the other languages have beautiful words: *Rose, Rosa, Gül*. If only because of your language, we have to kill you." They lament always being defined by minority conflicts and make jokes about it. Ronnie talks about his grandfathers, one Sephardic and one Ashkenazi, who despised each other. He quotes a Spaniolisch proverb, which one of them gave to the other: "He works and thus wastes time." Lively conversations about literature, film, theatre, and music. Ronnie says Istanbul is now the most intellectually exciting city (he has lived in London and New York). Claudia is very concerned about the political situation: no one knew what was really being played out. At any moment something could 'go off'. She is arranging a large reading tour of German authors in a bus as far as southern Anatolia and the Kurdish regions and cannot rule out dangerous incidents (said euphemistically). The beautiful Armenian peels an orange and hands a few slices to everyone at the table.

Istanbul, Monday, 1 December 2008

A drive along the Golden Horn to the rundown district of Fener. Everywhere abandoned houses, empty window openings, dismantled balconies, nailed-shut doors: the former, sometimes stately, homes of the Armenians and Greeks that, even if they can prove a claim of ownership, they will not be able to fix up again.

Somewhere in between, the Greek Orthodox Patriarchate. It was once the centre of Eastern Christianity and called itself the centre of the world. Until 1453 it was headquartered in the Hagia Sophia, then moved from church to church, which all burned down, until it found a modest home here: Aya Yorgi. The patriarch is still the head of the Greek Orthodoxy throughout the world. Four thousand believers still live here in Istanbul; at the time of the pogrom in 1955 there were two hundred thousand.

There are a few old icons from the Hagia Sophia, saved through the ages. A black pillar, said to have been used in the flagellation of Christ. (There is a similar one in Jerusalem.) On the images of the Child Jesus I notice for the first time the inscription OΩN (= ho ön, He Who is). It is the divine name revealed by Moses in the Septuagint translation (eimi ho ön), which we know in the form of 'sum qui sum' or 'I am who I am'. Is there a tradition in the Roman Church that the Son of God is ascribed the name of the Father? Is it a reminder of the dispute at the Council of Nicaea: is the Son of God of the same *substance* or only similar? The dispute over the one letter: the Iota.

In a small cafe nearby. Through the window a view of men sitting next to each other and looking forward, not talking to each other. Standing absentmindedly, two chew on their Simit bagels, one sweeps a hand occasionally through his hair. They do not seem depressed, they are not happy, not expecting or curious about anything. They simply look straight ahead. They see nothing in front of them that would be worth attention. Is that what *hüzün* looks like?

Many steep streets that lead to the Panagia Muhliotissa Church (or St. Mary of the Mongols, after the founder, a princess who was married to a Mongolian Khan and lived with him for fifteen years until he was assassinated), the only church not reclassified as a mosque. During the conquest of Constantinople this church, up on a mountain, had been impregnable. Mehmed II offered a compromise: if these Orthodox Christians subjected themselves to the Ottoman Empire, they could keep the church and also maintain their faith. The church dates from the thirteenth century, but there is nothing else worth noting about it. A few old icons, underneath them a sacred image in silver (Mary and Baby Jesus) with openings for the heads painted within them. The head of Jesus once again bears the three letters meaning 'He Who Is'. The church and the courtyard surrounding it are heavily secured. A heavy iron gate with a tiny flap which is opened by the gatekeeper – all we can see is her nose – who asks what we want. The fear of fundamentalist attacks is great. The Greek Church nearby is surrounded by fences a metre high.

To Chora Church, from the eleventh century, far outside the Byzantine city walls. ('Chora' means 'on the field'.) It lies like a jewel on a well-manicured plot between trees and meadows, and it is a museum. Almost like a mockery against the backdrop of abject Christian reality in this city. Strange pictorial inventions on the frescoes and mosaics from the life of Jesus. The nativity scene: Mary is in the middle, in a mandorla, at the bottom left two nurses care for the newborn. The Child is depicted once more above the reclining Mary, in a sort of bowl (a feed trough?) from which the heads of an ox and ass protrude. From the very top a broad ray leads into the tub. At the bottom right sits Joseph, aloof and sullen.

All self-contained scenes without a narrative sequence. The stark realism of the Bethlehem infanticide: a soldier hangs a child from the hand like a skinned rabbit; another plunges a sword into a child; an impaled infant on a tall spike; body parts hang from beneath the robes of a mother. The Anastasis Fresco shows Christ in hell as he pulls Adam and Eve out of the abyss simultaneously by the right and left wrist. Behind him, men and women swarm – the pushing and shoving of a mob addicted to redemption, who want to squeeze the hands of the Saviour through the eye of a needle.

By taxi – we travel all day by taxi – back 'to the city' ('Is tin polin', 'to the city', is said to have been the battle cry for the conquest of Constantinople, from which 'Istanbul' is derived) to Kalenderhane Camii. ('Kalender' was a Dervish order.) A Byzantine Cross Basilica, which is called either Diaconnissa Maria or Savior Kataleptos or Theotokos Kyriotissa (Theotokos). A big empty cube, the dome is supported by four high barrel vaults. We lie down on the carpet – no one gets lost here – and look up at the dome. The very bright church, flooded by a steady light, had a cycle of frescoes depicting the life of St. Francis, the oldest in the world, painted on the twenty-fifth anniversary of the saint's death. The artist has been called a proto Giotto, Ülker explains. (The frescoes were taken down after the whitewash had been removed.) I would like to know how the legend travelled so quickly to the Bosporus (certainly beyond Venice, but how did St. Francis fit into Orthodoxy?), and secondly, whether it is true that the St. Francis Portrait in the monastery at Subiaco Rome, generally considered the oldest 'realistic' portrait, not just of St. Francis, is older. Well, come to think of it, my drive for knowledge seems to have become quite out-of-date.

The Byzantine Summer Palace near Tekfur Sarayi is not open because of restoration work. Steep masonry walls. On the south side, double-arched windows high above, built of brick and marble alternating at regular intervals. This is reminiscent of Carolingian or Ottonian architecture. As well as the geometric patterns in the spandrels. But if the parallel is actually intended, it would be the reminder of the past perfect. As we approach the façade, which is not visible because of a wall, a large labrador barks at us angrily.

Tekfur Sarayi is now in a poor neighborhood. Under the imperial walls shabby and garishly dressed girls kick a dirty ball; boys play with fire in the grass; fat Turkish women sit on picnic benches chain smoking, cheerful and laughing together.

No men. We walk up a steep road with destroyed houses on the left and right and in front of us we hear a horrendous rant: a horde of teenagers shouting at a group of old and middle age women who bicker back with escalating voices. The boys, Ülker says, are using the usual swinish swear words of their generation, but from the mouths of the old women there sputters a flood of dirty, shameful, obscene words that she is too ashamed to translate, even if she knew the German words. An archaic scene: the ugly shrill voices of old women, who drive the men away with unspeakable words. The only thing missing was for them to bare their terrible vulvas, like the goddess Baubo in the Eleusinian ritual.

Istanbul, Tuesday, 2 December 2008

A taxi ride along the Bosphorus to the Villa Tarabya, which a Sultan had presented to Kaiser Wilhelm I, now part of the Federal Republic and the summer residence of the German ambassador. It is intended to hold the German-Turkish cultural academy, which is still to be founded. An 18 hectare site with landscaped gardens, a greenhouse, a tennis court and forest, all guarded by a large German shepherd. You do not want to encounter him without his master, the administrator. In the magnificent main house, the residence, the secret treaty of alliance between the German Reich and the Ottoman Empire was signed in August 1914. It prevented the Germans from intervening in the Young Turks' mass extermination of the Armenians, known by them down to the last detail through their ambassador, or at least protesting them.

We travel by boat to the Asian side of the Bosphorus, to Yeniköy. Over the water a high bank of fog thrusts itself out of the Black Sea, at first a few strands, then grows denser. It continues to spread to the southwest, and the villages – and the water around us – disappear. By taxi to Beykoz and Anadolu Kavagi, from where – the left and right of the road is a military zone (who do the Turks want to defend themselves from here?) – we drive high up into the mountains to a Genoese fortress with massive round towers constructed out of irregular ashlar rocks. The fortress was built as the 'gateway' to the Black Sea, and from up here you have the most panoramic view of the entire Pontus Euxine. But all we see is a single sea of fog, a closed blanket like clouds seen from the plane. And in the view of the surroundings, the billowing clouds strain and hurry over the oak and pine forests like those in paintings by Caspar David Friedrich. When Ülker suggested going out to the Black Sea, I thought of Ovid in Torni, of the Crimea, of Odessa with Isaac Babel and the giant stairway from *The Battleship Potemkin*. Perhaps these dream settings from early imagination were not destroyed by reality and a friendly muse has laid a veil over them. It is cold and damp up here, so quickly back to Anadolu Kavagi to catch the boat along the Bosphorus, but today because of the fog there are no more boats running. So we take a taxi back the long way on the Asian side.

We walk to the Egyptian spice bazaar – narrow streets, crowds, beguiling scents, calling, pointing merchants – and after much questioning and crossing back and forth finally find the stairs up to the small Rustem Paşa Camii, towering above the crowd like an oasis of tranquility sent down from heaven. Sounds rise up like distant memories. You can think your own thoughts. In front of the entrance a portico, a double row of eight columns, the capitals in the second row bearing the well-known muqarnas motif, while the ones in the front have a more stylised form. This shows that here Sinan 'plays' with a firmly fixed form predetermined by tradition to generate change, movement, and dynamism. I had not previously noticed this in his work. Inside, under the dome, four half spheres alternate with four arches, which forms an octagon. Above the mihrab two rows of three windows one above the other; beside them to the left and right two windows under arches. Four heavy octagonal buttresses in a square space. I had not seen such pure basic geometric shapes in Sinan before either – circle, semicircle, octagon, square – which combine to form an impression of a complete, simple, harmonious unit. At the north and south walls there are galleries, each with three arches outside. Through much coaxing – "The gentleman is a guest of the Ministry of Culture" – we are allowed into the galleries upstairs, where a completely different impression of the room emerges, the 'perceived' transition from circle to octagon, which is resolved below. The mosque is almost completely tiled over, cheerfully colourful. Among the colours the uncommon tomato or orange brown (the colour does not exist in nature); the secret of its production was lost after the sixteenth century. With binoculars I see that the calligraphy of the Holy name is also tiled; observed with the naked eye, it appears to be painted on. If you look at the tiles on top of the columns, you notice that they are not 'standardised' but appear to grow out of the capstones and bear only a few of the graphic elements from the regular tiles of the later period. Such details are hardly intended to be noticed; the impression of strict unity, the basic pattern, is deceptive. To me they are like the artist's allusion to the issue of transition: the rigorous geometric shape is not real; it grows out of isolated organic elements, which are then subjected to a unified, almost crystalline law. In the non-standard tiles Sinan has made the problem perceptible as a *process*. – Abundant light through the many windows everywhere, even in places where you would not normally find it. In the late afternoon sun, the light becomes a fairytale radiance on the tiles.

Istanbul, Wednesday, 3 December 2008

Travelling with Claudia and Fügen to Edirne, on the Bulgarian border, over the old military road to the Balkans, the road where the Suleiman's conquests began. The straight road is said to have been flanked by a variety of structures – caravanserais, hane, mosques – which were needed on the long road, but probably also represented the sovereign power. (It took a little longer than three hours for us to travel the distance; on horses, that would have been a ten-day ride.) Now the terrain can hardly be described as a landscape – desolate and empty, with sparse vegetation. Hazy skies. Halfway there we stop at a roadhouse. Colourful plastic toys, souvenirs (of what?), synthetic fibre kilims in garish colours, produced in Thailand. In the lobby there are leatherette chairs with leg rests. If you drop 2 lira into the armrest, the chair begins to vibrate and massages your back and legs.

Four towers suddenly appear in the distance; they rise abruptly from the ground to the sky, just like that: minarets, without the mosque or even any buildings we can see around them. As we get closer, the Selimiye Camii very gradually comes into view up on a mountain, and only then the lower lying city of Edirne, the old Adrianople, the capital of the Ottoman Empire before the conquest of Constantinople. From anywhere in the city the mosque can be seen hovering above – not crouching between houses as in other cities – between earth and heaven. It is Sinan's monumental work, the sum of his long life, the only one of his many mosques which he considered a masterpiece; the Süleymaniye was only an apprenticeship. He began the gigantic construction in 1568 at the age of seventy-eight, on behalf of Suleyman's successor, Selim II. It was initially built as a large caravanserai for the family, including the children and grandchildren, the servants, the structural engineers, stonecutters and labourers. The Selimiye was the only work that Sinan managed – for six years – during every phase of construction. It is said that he calculated the weight and volume of every single stone – marble, sandstone – himself. The mortar was mixed from eight different materials and was left to sit for a year, until it had reached a certain degree of hardness.

I notice when I enter the huge room that my pulse has quickened. It is a space defined by the dome, the largest he built, larger even than that of the Hagia Sophia. About 32 feet in diameter, 43 metres high – it does not just vault the room, but creates it. Around the perimeter of the dome the windows stand side by side, and on the walls under the arches the windows are both side by side and one above the other. All the light of the world enters here and seems no longer of this world. A man approaches; he wants to 'guide' me. I do not want to be guided; I do not want to do anything but look, but he does not give up. When he sees that I am looking up at the crown of the dome, he says: "There was a loose stone up there. When they took it out, there was a note behind it, written in Sinan's own hand: this stone came loose in the such-and-such-century, because the mass and shape are not exactly right (devious?) and it needs to be replaced. It came from the such-and-such-quarry ..." Is this true? Or is it one of the legends that was told by the master mason, who is still revered today? I ask the man if he could guide me into one of the four minarets. I want to see the three parallel, spiral staircases, the famous structural marvel I had read about in Moltke. I had jotted down a few sentences: "The minarets are more like pillars than towers, and yet they are so artificially constructed; three perfectly suitable staircases wind in its interior one into another, such that three people can climb at the same time." Moltke actually climbed them and counted 245 steps. "Without the least inclination towards vertigo, the first view from above seemed dreadful to me. It is believed that the terribly slender stone column could fall over if one approaches the edge of the gallery." I avoid every steeple, every mountain path with a precipice to the left or right, every highly perched vantage point, but I would like to climb up here. That would be quite impossible, the man says. No one was allowed inside or up there. I would have to send a request to Ankara; it could take months before it was dealt with, and it was questionable whether I would get a permit.

We are sitting in a cafe and observing the mosque from the outside. Again, the impression of a compact tortoise, as in the Süleimanye. Two galleries, narrow retaining walls with arched windows or half-domes in between. The slender minarets with their fluted columns and three balconies are (or were?) at 87 metres the highest in the world. The brown doves of the Prophet encircle the dome; above us tattered, swift white clouds; sun.

A gentleman stands there and observes us taking notes about the outer shell of the building. It turns out that he is from the city's Heritage Office. I say wistfully that I'd love to see the spiral staircases in the minarets, but had no permit. He pulls a key from his pocket, saying, "Come," and closes ranks on me. So fortunately I enter the base, which no one has obviously entered for a long time. Dust, decay. There are the entranceways to the three staircases that wind their way around each other so closely. I pace off the distance between the entranceways and it measures just 2 metres. The solid stone (küfekye, sandstone?) is supported by the shaft. I dare to climb one of the stairways up to the first balcony, and its exit – as well as its entrance – has been nailed shut because of disrepair. In fact, from my staircase the other two cannot be seen. So each of the three Müezzins climbed unseen by the others to his balcony upstairs and while meditating, could get ready for prayer. How was such a narrow stairway enclosure – the base measures 3.80 metres, the height up to the third balcony over 70 metres – possible at all to engineer and build? And the delicate, simple and unadorned towers have continued to stand, incredibly perpendicular, for almost half a millennium. (But a gracious God has prevented my ascent.)

"Until ten, twenty years ago," the gentleman from the Heritage Office says, "four times three (that is to say twelve) Müezzins climbed up five times a day, out onto the balconies, shouting prayers in all four directions of the compass." Can you imagine those magic voices with their microtones and non-synchronised singing high above the city? Not with our scales.

We drive through the bleak landscape back to Istanbul, the sun setting behind us. Farewell to Ülker, who has prepared a small meal in her apartment with its views over the Bosphorus to Leander's Tower. The water below is black, a few lit ferries are still crossing. Ülker gives me books about Sinan and a splinter of porphyry from the Hagia Sophia. Attached to it she has tied a USB drive with the journal and the digital photos. Yes, I will come back. Soon.

Mimar Sinan:
The Euclid of his Age

In the summer of 1911 a young Swiss architect, who later called himself Le Corbusier, travels to the Orient with a friend through the Balkans to Turkey, Edirne, Istanbul, and Bursa. In amazement he stands in front of the buildings, which are so different from everything he knows. He draws, photographs, keeps a journal: the mosques have maintained the same basic geometric shapes for centuries – circle, sphere, square, cube. "As the result of a decree, a man of great spirit has defined the essence of art for fifteen centuries and it abruptly soared to the greatest heights." The diversity of sameness.

The greatest of all the architects who designed mosques was Sinan, the incomparable, who re-established a centuries-old tradition and led it to its climax. Who is this Sinan, of whom no image has survived, no architectural treatise, not a single architectural drawing? Who had already become a legend in his own lifetime, and died at the age of one hundred? Of whom there exist a few letters to his Sultan, a few contradictory 'autobiographies,' of whom the poet Mustafa Sa'i, a young friend, wrote Oriental poetry in the language of flowers?

Sinan was born around 1490 in the village Agirnas in the Kayseri province Cappadocia. He was of Armenian (some say Greek, in any case Christian) origin and learned carpentry. At about twenty he was conscripted and sent to Istanbul for training as a Janissary. Such conscriptions of talented youths from ten to twenty were a common annual practice. They sought Albanians, Bulgarians, Bosnians, Greeks, and Armenians, but never Turks or Kurds.

He later called himself Yusuf Bin Abdullah (the common patronymic of converts), but he remained connected to his family and his village his entire life. When, after the conquest of Cyprus in 1572, the whole village (almost entirely Christians) was supposed to be relocated, he obtained authorisation for his family to stay. He remembered all of his relatives in his will, and donated a fountain to the village.

In Istanbul he received a thorough grounding in arithmetic and geometry, in languages (Ottoman Turkish, Arabic, Persian), in the Koran, in the types of weapons, in military technology and tactics. He was particularly interested in geometry and engineering arts such as hydraulics, which were based on the uninterrupted access to Greco-Roman sources. (During the Renaissance, they had to be labouriously gathered together again, without being supported by the centuries-old traditions of craftsmanship.)

Presumably he took part as a simple soldier in the campaigns of Selim I to Syria and Egypt (1516–17), then in the wars of Suleiman the Magnificent in Rhodes and Belgrade

(1521), Mohacs in Hungary (1526), Vienna (1529) Baghdad (1534–35), Corfu (1537), Apulia and Moldova (1538), to name the most important. In each of the campaigns he held a higher rank. (Promotion was carried out according to the 'merit system', not by religious affiliation or ancestry.) He progressed from cavalry officer to commander of novice and Janissary regiments, commanded the army of the 'Archers', who meanwhile carried muskets, and then soldiers with slingshots and mechanics. In the battle against the Safavids in Anatolia, he built three galleys that could carry heavy guns across Lake Van. In Moldova, he built a bridge in ten days over the Prut by anchoring the pillars into the water. (Earlier bridge builders had failed because they had tried to do it in the swamp land.) He built fortifications or demolished them. At the siege of Vienna, he was said to be the one who blasted a breach in the wall with improved catapults.

He commanded, fought, built, safeguarded the river crossings for the big battalions with their horses and heavy artillery – and he studied. He studied the Roman and Byzantine fountain and waterworks systems, studied ancient temples and palace ruins, he made note of pillars and stones for later transportation from the giant empire to Istanbul, including those of a palace that King Solomon had built for the Queen of Sheba in Cyzicus, on the Hellespont. He studied the mosque compounds with their madrasas, hospices, hospitals, sepulchral monuments, minarets, caravanserais, and hammams, and learned what his predecessors could and could not do. It was always the domes that interested him. Would they not let themselves build any wider and higher in order to at least approximate the unsurpassed, albeit vulnerable, dome of Hagia Sophia?

In 1537 Sinan was appointed chief royal architect. This required superhuman organisational skills: overseeing four dozen other architects, as well as those from the major cities of the empire and the conquered provinces, who wanted their building projects examined, modified and possibly approved. The supervision of the width and paving of streets, the height of the houses and their demolition, if necessary, to make room for official buildings. The supervision of the workshops: carpenters, brick and lime kiln workers, bricklayers, masons, marble cutters, crate and tile makers, ink manufacturers, painters, plasterers, calligraphers, glaziers, blacksmiths, block and tackle manufacturers, metal workers (for domes), tilers, surveyors, ground and water workers, and galley slaves. The submission of designs, including alternatives, the cost calculation for the structures (materials, transport, labour) and financial negotiations. Supervision of the construction sites, sometimes in several places of the empire at the same time.

Before anything could be built at all, the underground water systems usually had to be created first. (The Byzantines had abandoned the ingenious supply system of the Romans over the centuries and were content with cisterns, but the Muslims needed running water for their ablutions.) This required:

unearthing the systems from the time of the infidels, creating new main lines, building distribution chambers, inflows and outflows, dams, weirs, aqueducts, water towers, stations, manholes, the computation of currents and stress, and protection against floods. For the biggest new water system, the Kirkçesme, which took ten years to build, he drew the water from two lakes in Thrace, from the so-called 'Belgrade Forest', 25 kilometres north of Istanbul, and conducted it into the city over four aqueducts. The line supplied the huge Süleymaniye complex and afforded the city three hundred fountains with running water.

The first major mosque he built was for the young, deceased crown prince Mehmed, the Şehzade Mehmed Camii (1544–48). The wise and popular prince had succumbed to a fever at 21 years old, somewhere in the province he served as governor. Sultan Süleyman is said to have wept for two and a half hours at the news, then fasted and prayed for forty days and nights. After the death, the question of succession was unclear; the Sultan wanted one of the surviving sons, and the Janissaries wanted the other.

The choice of the site for the mosque complex was strategic: on the cusp of the third of the seven hills, on whose other end the Hagia Sophia and Topkapi Palace stood, at the edge of high aqueduct of Valens, "a Byzantine spectre... with its long form resembling a liner..." (Le Corbusier) whose water Sinan had to route with an inverted siphon, with views down to the

Golden Horn and the Bosphorus and across to the regions inhabited by the Genoese and other infidels who inhabited Pera. It was a new idea in urban planning for this city, as there was no higher lying mosque, so it changed the silhouette of the city. And it was politically motivated, because the old barracks of the Janissaries, which had to be partially demolished, were located on the grounds.

The mausoleum was already completed when Sinan began the construction of the mosque complex. Animals were sacrificed and the meat distributed to the poor. The floor plan shows two equal squares – a marble-paved courtyard and a mosque – which are connected by two minarets, each with two balconies. The dome (with a circle of windows) sits exactly in the middle and was immediately perceived by his contemporaries as the climax and completion of existing dome architecture. It rests on four polygonal columns and is supported by four half-domes, also windowed, at whose corners four round towers stand halfway between the dome and half-domes as extensions of the pilasters, which unifies the exterior and the interior. In the extension of the diagonal axes, the four exedrae are in front of the towers, which broadens the volume of the building. In front – broader, deeper – galleries with arched windows under round arches, and in front of that – even deeper and broader – archways with small domes over a pair of arched doorways on small columns.

The whole when viewed from one of the façades – you see the entire structure, because there is enough space around it, as if it is on stage – looks like an elegant, descending pyramid. (With the reminder perhaps of the yurt tents of nomadic peoples starting out on the steppes.) A single, compact, harmonious unit from which nothing distracts, composed of basic geometric shapes. Solid yet light at the same time and brightened by the interior openings, the archways and the galleries, which, ironically, are there to conceal the severity of the support structures behind them. Only now did I notice the paradox: the heaviness of the dome above, the lightness of the pillars below, and how by this lightness the heaviness begins to lift and float.

The two slender minarets are unique in their ornamental variety: vertical stripes of stars, rosettes, crescent moons, knot motifs. Muqarnas crowns complete the balconies, a trickling of stalactites. Everything is easy, playful, cheerful, youthful. Süleymaniye's minarets will be strict and austere.

Inside: a great height, through the many rows of windows lining all sides a light-flooded, weightless emptiness. Nothing presses down on you: the massive hexagonal pillars above, fluted where they meet the half-domes, dissolving, so to speak, into the arches of alternating coloured stone that support the dome floating above its crown of windows. From the apex of the dome, above the heads of the worshipers, hang two simple, extensive rings of oil lamps. When they looked up, the worshipers, it is said that in the lights they see the sparkle of the stars in the sky and above the vault of heaven. The mosque as the reflection of the universe.

"When the foundations of the mosque were laid, the structure slowly rose from the ground like effervescent bubbles on the sea of elegance, with its multicoloured domes soaring up towards heaven like the rainbow," a contemporary wrote.

The floor plan of the Şehzade complex has a madrasah almost as big as the squares of the district court and the mosque, an elementary school, a hospice, and a caravanserai with stables. The mausoleum for the prince has been tiled all over in springtime colours. Through its windows you can look out into the garden, as if into paradise.

No sooner had the mosque complex for the heir been completed than the Sultan wanted to have his own – even bigger, even more magnificent, even closer to the Golden Horn, the entire silhouette of the third hill transformed and henceforward dominant, once more a political-theological demonstration of power for the unbelievers on the opposite Pera shore. (Süleyman was 56 years old, and he had ruled for 36 years; during his reign the kingdom was the strongest economic and military power in the world. Now he was ailing, strict, ascetic, and pious.)

For the vast site houses and whole streets, the Janissary barracks, parts of the old palace and the garden were once again demolished. It was necessary to elevate the terrain because it was sloping and steep in many places towards the Horn, to secure it. Each of these spots were supported by substructures on top of vaults, on which later, layered below, outbuildings

– schools, shops, and the caravanserai were built. (The domes high above would soar up from dome-shaped structures deep below.) The construction of the compound has been called the largest undertaking of the Ottoman Empire other than the campaigns. When the site was finished, Sinan submitted the plan once more to the Sultan and his dignitaries, demonstrated, discussed new desires. Then, in the presence of notables, he staked off the area with posts and ropes, and the engineers, 'experts in geometry,' began to dig the foundations. It took three years of construction for the foundation and another year to prepare the stones, mainly sandstone from the surrounding area. The Sultan came once more with his court at an hour which astrologers calculated as auspicious – animals were sacrificed, alms distributed, and the Grand Mufti Ebussuud laid the foundation for the Mihrab "with his blessed hands".

It took six architects to procure antique columns and marble for Sinan. He knew from his campaigns exactly what he wanted, and at the same time this was a highly symbolic act, because in his desire to compete at least with the Hagia Sophia he was following the practice of Justinian. He sent for columns from Alexandria, the Temple of Jupiter in Baalbek, from Anatolia, Alanya, Silifke, Thessaloniki, Nicaea, Miletus, and Mitilini (Lesbos), in addition to wood and lead from Northern Greece and the Black Sea, iron for the cramps and support rods from Bulgaria. 'Sent for' is easily said. For the transport of four monolithic granite columns from Alexandria a special quay with wood from the forests of Thrace had to be set up, in addition to two heavy transport ships, built by shipping companies in the Dardanelles. Other ships for the columns out of Baalbek, which had been dragged across Lebanon on sleds.

The labour force. The giant empire was so well organised that it was known which experts were to be found in which city. So orders went out to the Kadis for a number of carpenters, metal workers, and quarrymen, and to provide marble cutters from time to time, with the particular person assuming responsibility for the number. Then there was the conscription of forced labour from the conquered provinces; there were the galley slaves and the novices. Religious affiliation did not matter. The excavation workers were almost all non-Muslims, as were the majority of masons and blacksmiths. Most of the carpenters, painters, glaziers and lead specialists were Muslims. The bookkeeping was meticulous, as can be seen by the fact that on the weekend two and a half to three thousand artisans and workers had to be paid. (No more than eighty builders a day are said to have worked on the Christian cathedrals.) Wages were also paid to the slaves and forced labourers, because not to do so would have diminished the Sultan's merit in building a work pleasing to God. After completion of the Süleymaniye, four hundred slaves who had worked on it received their freedom.

The Hagia Sophia, against which all mosque builders are measured, has a very rough exterior, which surrounds the jewel of the interior like a cage. Sinan, on the other hand, did not want the interior to be shielded from "the world outside", but instead integrated the interior and exterior, creating a unity of repeated reflections inside.

> An elementary geometry orders these masses: the square, the cube, the sphere. In plan it is a rectangular complex with a single axis. The orientation of the axis of every mosque on Moslem soil toward the black stone of the Kaaba is an awe-inspiring symbol of the unity of the faith.
>
> (Le Corbusier)

> The pyramidal composition of the exterior architecture possesses a dynamism that veritably 'erupts' from within. Here the roofing system consists of domes of various sizes. Arranged at different levels below the main dome, they reveal a movement like that of waves rising and falling around a rock. The simple geometry of this dynamic exterior architecture has no parallel anywhere in world architecture...
>
> (Dogan Kubon)

... One could believe it was built on a mountain and grew to an absurd size in one night. The white sanctuary

expands its domes through its large cubes of masonry,
within its own 'city' of stone.

(Le Corbusier)

Outside: the series of arcades below allow the heavy mass of
the building above to disappear in their shadow. The large supporting pillars are balanced by the rhythm of the small arcade
arches with their graceful columns. It is the same idea used
in the Şehzade, but monumentalised. And it seems that the
opportunity to work with shadows did not come to him till
here.

Inside: every corner is bright, but not glaringly light. There
are filters in the windows to prevent direct sunlight – wide
diffuse light, so there are no shadows. On the walls, above
doors, above and below windows there is calligraphy in different font types and sizes: the Holy name, verses from the
Koran, for example from the Verse of Light: "God is the light
of the heavens and the earth ... light upon light – God guides
/ to His light whomever He wants" (Rueckert). But, they say,
the worshippers could not read the ancient Arabic characters (or else, most often, could not read at all), they saw only
abstract, mysterious, perhaps magical shapes. In this way God
(unlike in our fine churches) was placed almost perceptibly in
the background. Again, there is a contrast like that between
heaviness and lightness: light upon light for every believer and
at the same time an inability to comprehend God's ways. Le
Corbusier called the mosque a huge "sphinx-like apparition".

We climb up here from the water on a May evening, walking up steep winding streets and alleys with the substructures for the vast plateau resting beneath them, walking to Sinan's tomb outside the walls of Kulliye, the mosque complex, over and around the wall to the south side. A small restaurant has opened and they serve us the traditional bean dish. From here, looking straight through the cypress trees, you have one of the few frontal views of one of the façades and of the dome. The Süleymaniye crouches there in the twilight like an ancient animal. Closed, enigmatic, mysterious. Like the memory of bad dreams that seem to stand as still as clouds and would accompany you your entire life. In some dreams, we know: this is not a dream. As it is now.

> There is a silence that only one who has *heard* it can
> imagine.
>
> (Le Corbusier)

How did the voices of the Imam, the prayer leaders, the Friday sermon, sound in the vast rooms? The hydraulic engineer had figured out the laws of acoustics. He understood the frequency of sound waves, and made sure that they had no direct contact with regular shapes such as smooth wall surfaces. The waves should be able to spread out evenly, without stopping, without superimposition of frequencies. He used niches, buttresses, and balustrades with advanced, barely visible perforated marble slabs, and sometimes used soft and elastic types of plaster. The most obvious, when you first know about it, is the use of the muqarnas to break the sound waves into different sizes on the walls, through doors, in the corners, this concave, gently stepped, tiered stalactite-motif on the equilateral triangle, which sometimes stands on the apex and sometimes on the foundation. Everywhere. You admire it like jewelry, like an ornament, while at the same time it has a precisely calculated acoustic function. By the same token, there are also sound amplifiers in the domes, aligned with the voices; terracotta hollows behind small, engraved grates. Sixty-four such amplifiers were installed in the great dome of the Suleymaniye, but to the eye they appear as nothing more than stimulating jewelry.

The system of acoustics is thoughtfully designed in Sinan's mosques, planned like those of the structural engineering and aesthetics. No structure exists 'for itself'; it also exists for others, which it both depends on and supports. And the even distribution of the sound corresponds to the uniform distribution of light.

Of counting and measuring. The architects of the Italian Renaissance used geometric and arithmetic units, the circle and circle segment, square, rectangle, hexagon, octagon for the ground plan, numerical ratios for the surface area. The order of the world was based on numbers and their relationships to each other, as well as the intervals of tones and the proportions of the human body. This order should be reflected in the sacred buildings, as a unified system of mathematical relations, as harmony of all the parts ('disposition' in the words of Vitruvius), as a geometric and arithmetic ratio of the parts to one another and to the whole ('symmetria').

What information there was, since Pythagoras, was made famous by Plato's 'Timaeus', by Euclid, Vitruvius, Boethius, and you could look it up in the numerous architectural treatises, often written by the builders themselves, and review the attached plans.

There is not one architectural treatise from the Ottomans, not a single architectural drawing that has been preserved. What did Sinan know? How did he plan? It is assumed that he knew the ancient sources, especially Vitruvius, and it is true that he repeatedly studied the Hagia Sophia and studied the problem of the free-standing dome, had examined and sometimes repaired numerous mosques in the vast empire of Budapest to Mecca and Jerusalem. But did he know – more than just hearsay from Italian travellers – that Brunelleschi, Bramante, Michelangelo, and Palladio faced problems with domes similar to his own, which he sometimes resolved in a more daring way than the Italian masters? Did he know that the largest church in Western Christendom was being produced in Rome at the same time he was building the largest mosque of Islam, the Süleymaniye, in Constantinople, the second Rome?

The geometric and arithmetic fundamentals were the same. But there were modules added during the construction of mosques that, to the Western mind – based on everything

160

we know – were foreign. The Arabic characters, like the Hebrew, have a numerical value (Alif =1, Ba = 2), and the addition of the letters produces a mystical-magical number, which results, for example, in a name. In the name as number a hidden meaning beyond the sum of its letters is revealed. And this meaning is related to the cosmos, ordered through numbers. So the numerical value of Allah is 66, Mohammed is 92, Ali, Muhammad's son-in-law, is 110, Mussa (Moses) is 116. There are different starting points: the number of letters of the alphabet (32), the sum of the suras of the Koran (114). The name of Sultan Suleyman is identical, by its numeric value (191) to King Solomon, whose temple he wanted to surpass in size. Sinan used such figures and dividers or multipliers to calculate his modules: for the length, height and depth of the stones, for walls, windows and doors, pillars, the height of domes and their diameters, measured according to the value of the Ottoman Elle (1 arsine = 75.7738 cm) and its divisors after the 24th and the 60th system. So the measurements of the stones, the distances, and the heights of the Rüstem Pasha Mosque repeatedly symbolise the name of Allah and Ali in their numerical value. With one exception: the niche in front of the side entrance next to the minaret is built according to the module of the name Sinan (161). In that is expressed the self-assertion of an artist beyond his serving role.

Sinan's mastery is demonstrated by the fact that the geometric and arithmetic modules are almost always congruent. Our untutored eye, of course, can only see the geometry. But it is a peculiar, rapturous feeling, to stand in spaces that are constructed out of the Holy name, out of whose letters the world has been created.

According to tradition, every mosque has a circle of surrounding buildings. There had never been as many as those at the Suleymaniye before: five madrasahs (a primary school, and four classroom buildings where mathematics, astronomy, and later law and theology were taught). The vaulted cells of the madrasa march in military formation down to the water. From these buildings of teaching and learning there are many views, always diagonal, of the mosque. (Who is able to look head-on?) Next: a medical college including a teaching hospital, an asylum overlooking trees and flowers (while at the same time in Europe the insane were exhibited like zoo animals), the bakery, the large kitchen, and a dining room for scholars, students and the poor, built around a large square garden where we could sit and drink apple tea, since alcohol is forbidden in the sacred precinct. There is also a guest house for distinguished guests including a caravanserai below it for the animals. Here, rather austere despite its size, the old Islamic traditions found their most generous, functional and precisely well-reasoned, but never opulent, expression: education, charity, hospitality.

The cost of building the complex, including the cost of maintenance, consisted of the tax revenue taken from 221 villages, 7 mills, 2 locks, 2 islands, 30 arable fields, 2 harbours etc., collected by 30 tax collectors. The cost of transport (from

162

Alexandria, Baalbek, Thrace, etc.) was to be shouldered by the respective provincial governors.

The cost of the complex and the Süleymaniye Kirkçyesme water system were about the same. As Sinan handed over the keys of the completed mosque to Süleyman, Süleyman gave them back to him: he, the master builder, should unlock his work.

While the Süleymaniye complex was being built, he built a mosque in Damascus for his master at the same time, and a double bathhouse in the form of two huge dice for his wife, Hürrem Sultan, at the Hagia Sophia. Immediately after that the small, delightfully tiled Rüstem Pasha Mosque above the spice bazaar (accessible by two lateral symmetrical staircases), a mosque for the Sultan's daughter Mihrimah, caravanserais, public baths, and waterworks.

Then, from 1567 to 1568, when he was in his late seventies, he succeeded with another stroke of genius: the famous bridge Büyük Çekmece on the road to Edirne, the high road to the Balkans. It spanned a wide lagoon where, during a hunting expedition, the Sultan had just barely escaped drowning by a hair's breadth. The height and speed of the water were erratic, and previous attempts to bridge it were immersed in the swamp and marsh land. He laid the bridge out alongside the entrance to the Sea of Marmara (where the lagoon opens out), where the water is shallow and the ground firm, created three artificial islands, barely higher than the water surface, to support the weight of the bridge from one island to another with the help of the arches, temporarily pumping off the water with hundreds of other workers "and with the help of spirits and demons" in order to ram in three man-sized wooden piles under each proposed support, so the stone foundations, bound together with iron clamps, came to rest on the arches. The bridge (more precisely, four bridges) is 635 metres long and so wide that there was room for two caravans to pass each other side by side. In one of his 'autobiographies' Sinan writes: "This heavenly bridge was a marvel of the age. The world conqueror congratulated his wretched slaves and traveled, greatly pleased, further on his train to Szigetvar." (Where he died.) Büyük Çekmece is the only one of Sinan's structural works which is mentioned on his grave stone.

Sinan has called Şehzade his apprentice work, the Süleymaniye his journeyman's piece. The Selimiye in Edirne, the old capital of Adrianopel, was going to be his masterpiece. When he began to build it he was 78 years old; when he completed it, he was 85.

> Adrianople appears in the splendor of full afternoon
> light. Adrianople is like a swelling on this vast plateau,
> culminating in a magnificent dome. Tremendous
> minarets, in the distance as delicate as marsh horsetails,
> emphasize and direct this great thrust upright... The
> Sultan Selim gives the city a tiara of great splendor.
>
> (Le Corbusier)

The Selimiye grows out of the land – from a distance the minarets and the dome stand alone on the horizon – just as the mosques of Istanbul grow out of the city.

The gigantic dome is crowned by eight hexagonal towers with pointed metal caps; the four graceful, towering minarets do not stand, as usual, separately; they are directly connected to the mosque, are integrated at the corners of the base square into the complex. The whole is one big push, surge, thrust upward.

The poet Sa'i wrote: "The four minarets, like the four companions of the Prophet (namely the four Sunni caliphs), are the glory of the world; the dome is an allusion to the light of the religion of the prophets."

Inside: the *pure* dominance of the dome (as only in the Pantheon), establishing a single monumental space which is detected at a glance. Why does it seems to float and yet hold everything together at the same time? It is built on an octagon of fluted buttresses that do not – as columns usually do – stand in the room and block the view, but come out of the walls and are interconnected by semicircular arcs. This bears the weight of the pillars, which are only half-height, but massive. And they resolve in the capitals with the muqarnas motif, which continues airily – a circle of thirty-two windows – between and above the arches, in the interstices, to the top of the dome. The transition from circle to octagon is not noticeable; there is a single, great downward momentum, and yet at the same time it seems that the higher up you look, the more the heaviness evaporates.

While Sinan built the dome, he repaired (how many times?) the dome of the Hagia Sophia, which he had vied with his entire life, and which he now believed, with the Selimiye, he had surpassed. Sa'i has handed down a passage from the master builder: "Who among Christians who considers himself an architect, claims that in the Ottoman Empire no dome would rival that of the Aya Sophia, that no Islamic architect would be able to build such a large dome. In this mosque, with the help of Allah and Sultan Selim, I have built a dome 6 ells wider and 4 ells higher (the Ottoman ell equals 75.7738 cm) than the Aya Sophia." Is that true? Since the dome of the Hagia Sophia is difficult to measure because of its slightly elliptical shape, there are various calculations. Some say he surpassed it; others deny it. (The dome of the Selimiye has a diameter of 31.50 m., the Hagia Sophia has a major axis of 30.90 m., and a minor axis of 31.82 m.) Are a few centimetres more or less important, or are they just one example of the ambition, or no – the mastery – finally reached by the architect? But at the same time also the evidence of religious-political triumph? The Selimiye should, after Selim's conquest of Cyprus in 1570/71, also symbolise the victory of Islam over Christianity (which was again called into question by the battle of Lepanto in October 1571).

Sa'i sees mirrored in this dome the dome of heaven, equally weightless – 'columnless' – hovering above us.

Exactly in the middle, under the dome – common in a mosque – stands a square platform for the muezzin to lean on, by arched, interconnected pillars. Exactly in the middle, underneath it, on the other hand, stands an octagonal marble fountain with a square outer frame. Above it, on the ceiling (that is to say, on the underside of the platform) the wheel of heaven is painted as a circular vortex. Here, on the axis mundi in the navel, the omphalos of the prayer room, the geometry of the building is repeated – circle, octagon, square – as if it were almost an earthly glimpse of the vertical axis of the celestial dome.

Some have compared the Selimiye with the Rock in Jerusalem, which Sinan had once repaired. It also has an octagonal structure that surrounds the sacred rock, from which the Prophet ascends on his horse into the sky. From it the throne of God will descend on the Day of Judgment. The omphalos in the prayer room should be thought of as this rock.

The triumphant mihrab, constructed of Marmara marble, easily breaks through the wall, like a pseudo apse, as if it were already in another world. It is decorated with colourful Iznik tiles – flower gardens, flowering trees, spring. A Garden of Eden, Sa'i called it. The calligraphy on the mihrab – the first, the opening sura, Al-Fatiha – was, with its rhythmically flowing letters, for Sa'i the river of Paradise.

An early admirer writes about Selimiye: "Such things do not exist in the world; beauty and elegance are beyond description."

I wondered, and still wonder, why Sinan's art cannot be described. Because it does not 'explain'? Because it is only dimensional limitations that can illustrate the solutions to technical problems? "Instead of empathy: abstraction." (Le Corbusier) The problem of representation without explanation is solved in mathematical language. And 'The Art of Fugue' would not be characterised any differently. If you know how something is made, does that tell you anything about the state of being overwhelmed? About the beauty?

After Selimiye he built five more mosques, madrasahs, caravanserais, mausoleums, soup kitchens, and the bridge over the Drina in Bosnia. In 1583, at age ninety-four, he set out on the pilgrimage to Mecca. He was already a living legend – the Euclid of his age – but, in keeping with his status, his palace servants remained by his side. He died with more than a hundred.

His grave, outside the Süleymaniye, is in the shape of an open circle.

References
Attila Arpat, 'Modulare Ordnung und symboüsche Zahlen in den Abmessungen der Rüstem Paşa Moschee', in:

Uluslararast Mimar Sinan, Sempozyumu Bildiirileri,
Ankara 1966, pp. 205–216.

Augusto Romano Barelli/Paola Sonia Gennara, *Die
Moseltee von Sinan,* Wolfgang Voigt, Deutsches
Architekturmuseum frankfurt, Tübingcn: Wasmuth,
2008.

Hans G. Egli, *Sinan. An Interpretation,* Istanbul: ege
yayainlari, 1997.

Godfrey Goodwin, 'Sinan, Light and Form', in: *Uluslararast,*
pp. 217–220.

Mutbul Kayili, 'Sinan's Acoustical Technology', in:
Uluslararast, pp. 171–177.

Dogan Kuban, *Ottoman Architecture,* Woodbridge, Suffolk:
Antique Collectors' Club, 2010.

Le Corbusier, *Reise nach dem Orient,* Giuliano Gresleri,
Zürich: Spur Verlag, 1991.

Le Corbusier, *Journey to the East,* Ivan Żaknić, Cambridge/
Mass.: MIT Press, 2007.

Gülru Necipoğlu, *The Age of Sinan,* London: Reaktion
Books, 2005.

J. M. Rogers, *Sinan,* London: I. B. Tauris (Oxford Centre for
Islamic Studies), 2006.

Something about Kilims

to and fro in shadow from inner to outer shadow

Samuel Beckett

At first glance, there is a colourful area which contains seemingly regular geometric figures. Triangles, squares, diamonds, rectangles, hexagons. Strange patterns, composed of basic geometric shapes that might have meaning. Zigzags in the water. Toothed vertical strands like zippers, where stepped figures – small squares – criss-cross each other. Six triangles make one star, and in the middle a different coloured double triangle has been knitted. (A central bar runs through the star beyond this point, which makes the pattern look like a spindle.) These and similar patterns can be found on all kilims. There are archaic forms like those on early ceramics and pottery, and that means these flat woven or knitted fabrics are as old as the domestication of sheep and goats. They have maintained their variety of shapes over the centuries, millennia, because apart from the development of the sacred and art production of the civilisations on their nomadic wanderings and in the villages of Central Asia, the Caucasus and Anatolia, were produced for everyday use, such as saddle blankets, supply bags, tent decorations, curtains for protection against the weather, and pillows, but never as carpets.

What is it about these knitted fabrics that so fascinates us today? Morton Feldman, the American composer, suggested that only modern painting – he names Matisse – and music (Stravinsky, Varese, Steve Reich) have opened our eyes to this 'disproportionate symmetry'. This is due to the way the kilims are constructed; in that process we are drawn into contemplation if we follow the irregularity in the regular. The flat weave fabric is not a knotted rug, which requires that you work out the details of the fixed pattern or design in certain length and width in advance. The weave, in contrast, is 'open', to some extent improvised.

The production method is very simple. Two stakes are driven into the ground and the warp threads – often from sheep's wool – are suspended between them on a string. (Sometimes, though rarely, the scratchy goat hair from which the Bedouin tents are woven, is also used, despite the fact that this is supposed to have been how the kilim got its name, a word borrowed from the late Greek, *Kilikia*, for the wool of the Cilician goats.) From weft threads or weft yarn the surfaces and patterns are woven with the warp. The front and back sides are often the same or mirrored, because, unlike a knotted rug, there is no underside. Although the kilim is usually bought with the framing and borders as a unified, single piece, its design is never ending, without beginning, middle and end, continuing like a piece of serial art, like the early art of Frank Stella.

The weaver folded up the knitted fabric along with the stakes when the family moved on, drove them into the ground again at the next camp and continued with her *work in progress*. But she did not want to weave along mechanically; she wove as she liked. So the *process* of weaving becomes visible. The distances between the patterns are not equal, and these may be sometimes larger, sometimes smaller than before. Some patterns do not appear at all, others in their place, or a surface remains empty. Sometimes the number and arrangement of the patterns are the same, but they appear in a different colour. This may be related to the mood of the weaver, but maybe it is more a matter of the availability of the material.

Extracting colour from the native plants was a lengthy process and the quantity is not very abundant, so there was a need to dye over and over again, resulting in the most subtle nuances. Only by the colour, not by the patterns, which are used everywhere, can a trader tell where the carpet was knit, because they know what plants are native, or were available there. This applies to the villages and centres like Bergama (Pergarnon) Adyama, Malatia, Konya, Diyarbakir, and Adana. It is more difficult, on the other hand, to identify the nomad kilims. On the long, wandering trek there were perhaps entirely different plants, and the colours of the knitted fabrics inevitably changed. What seems arbitrary, 'incoherent' in view of what has previously been woven, has its basis in the coincidence of existing material; it is a different type of 'composition' than that of sedentary people, a somewhat free improvisation, often in no way related back to those that already existed. (Feldman writes, there is the feeling of something immediately imminent or at hand – "something imminent. And what is imminent, we find, is neither the past nor the future, but simply – the next ten minutes. The next ten minutes. We can go no further than that, and we need go no further.") The nomads knitted fabrics that are indefinable, 'indeterminable'. (Can we say, following a spontaneous inspiration?) The traces of wandering are woven into them. If we knew more about the geography of the early, no doubt long lost, plants, we could with help reconstruct the fabric using the old methods, methods that were even older than Islam, where the rare, albeit abstracted human and animal figures clarify what does not exist in the Saracenic ornamentation. (The abstraction can go so far that we only see a geometric band, until the experts enlighten us: "Those are running dogs".)

"Given a very small inventory of basic ornamental forms the infinite capacity for variation, that two nomadic carpets will never look exactly the same, can be explained in large part by the diversity of the environments producing the colours." (So the Viennese art historian Alois Riegl, the author of the famous work *Die Spätrömische Kunstindustrie* (*Late Roman Art Industry*), and some writings on *Altorientalische Teppiche*

(*Old Oriental Rugs*). He has shown, for example, that black borders are 'intuitively' reminiscent of the late antique mosaic.)

The colours: this oriental colourfulness of *The Arabian Nights*. They have over time lost little of their luminosity (like the colours in Egyptian burial chambers, where kilims are also represented): *Crocus sativus*, the saffron, *Isatis tinctoria*, the indigo-coloured woid, *Indigofera tinctoria*, the alkanet (*Alkanna tinctoria*), the ruby red colour, and still used to extract a yellow-reddish dye for Henna – "for the fingernails and the back of women's hands". Especially krapp, the branched, deep root of the madder plant (*Rubia tinctorum*) which was used to produce madder crimson, madder red, madder orange, and all the nuances ranging from pink to black-red, from purple to brown shades, including the most ardent: Turkish red. A variation is alizari, or smyrnaische krapp (*Rubia peregrina*) whose tint ranges from pink to fiery red, purple to black. And from woid and alkanna the triumphal glowing green is created: the Prophet's green.

I look at my kilim on the wall, a madder red surface where a few S symbols are scattered, which now seem to me to be less like symbols of luck than apotropaic characters. A single red and no red at all. From the carpet on the wall "unheard footfalls only sound". Sounds of colour in many shades of red; muted, closed sounds that are (almost) always identical. If I look carefully, the colour divides, the red is colourless and exuberant (another type of exuberance than luxuriance) at the same time. Micro sounds, or maybe the exhalation of the weft threads.

Colours and patterns in a dynamic relationship to one another; sometimes the colour is dominant, sometimes the pattern sequence. Sometimes a pattern seems to have disappeared from a row, and then you discover it again, hidden by the scarcely distinguishable colour of the surface, which is very different from the changing colours of the rows, but at the same time highlighted by a garish frame, which both attracts and deflects attention to itself. Some patterns appear 'reciprocal', which means that they spring into view like the front and back of a cube drawn in three dimensions: are these red serrated diamonds on white hexagons or are they white X shapes on a red background? Is that supposed to be black ironwork – like that on chests, (but where would nomads have gotten chests?) – dominating the surface on both sides of the knitted fabric, or is the white fretwork around the black the dominant, which encloses the large void and emerges as the more prominent? Such questions will never be answered; they remain in limbo. Only this is especially relevant, that flat woven fabric can have a deep impact.

In most kilims it suffices to see just a part (as in paintings or pictures in books); even when a different section contains more or fewer patterns, more or fewer colours: it shows 'the whole'. In such a way can the whole work can be derived from a single sentence of *Finnegans Wake*. "Likewise, the character of Stravinsky's patterns (der Muster) does not seem to differ if a work of his is either long or short." Feldman writes, "Music and the designs or a repeated pattern (die Entwürfe) in a rug have much in common. Even if it be asymmetrical in its placement, the proportion of one component to another is hardly ever substantially out of scale (disproportionate) in the context of the whole. Most traditional rug patterns remain the same size when taken from a larger rug and adapted to a smaller one." And vice versa. The patterns, therefore, stand in principle for themselves, and are not each considered in proportion as parts to each other and are still, more or less, perceived as a whole – but: what constitutes the whole? "As a composer, I see on the other hand, that the sum of the parts does not equal the whole". (Karl von Foerster expressed that once this way: "The whole is different than the sum of its parts".)

Feldman recalled that John Cage had developed a music in the early fifties, in which all the parts, all the parameters, were independent of one another, were composed autonomously, according to laws that at any one time are randomly determined. Cage's music "...is not involved with the grammar of design," (the composer's 'idea') "and is perhaps the only music known to us in which concepts of symmetry/asymmetry cannot be applied." This balance is difficult to establish when one is compelled to follow conventional notation, in the face of Western music, which amounts to paraphrases of memory (Erinnerung). How can memory or the act of remembering 'be served' and circumvented at the same time, like the kilim? In a piano piece, 'Triadic Memories', Feldman had attempted to *formalise*, by repetition of particular chords that do not follow *apart from* each other, but *on top of* each other, then repeating the earlier ones again, a "disorientation of memory", as he writes. In this way it is *suggested* that what is heard is directed and functional, but that is just an illusion – because of varying duration, slight accelerations or retardations – "like walking the streets of Berlin – where all the buildings look alike, even if they're not." How does Feldman come to bring this repetition and its perceived directionality into balance ("beckoned back and forth and turned away")?

Feldman describes a small kilim from an Anatolian village with white tile patterns in a diagonal repetition of large stars in lighter reds, greens and beiges. "Everything about the rug's colouration, and how the stars are drawn in detail, when the rectangle of a tile is even, how the star is just sketched (as if drawn more quickly), when a tile is uneven and a little bit smaller – this, as well as the staggered placement of the pattern, brings to mind Matisse's mastery of his seesaw balance between movement and stasis. Why is it that even asymmetry has to look and sound right?" The colour-scale of most kilims appears more extensive than it actually is, because of the large variation in shades of the same colour (the abrash), which is linked to the small quantities of yarn obtained in the dyeing process. "As a composer, I respond to this most singular aspect of a microchromatic overall hue" ("heedless of the way, intent on the one gleam or the other"). "My music has been influenced mainly by the methods in which colour is used on essentially simple devices. It has made me question the nature of musical material. What could best be used to accommodate, by equally simple means, musical colour? Patterns."

The question of patterns recalls Cage's demand made on the music: to imitate nature "in the manner of its operations". No one leaf is like another. They are more or less the same and somehow different. Like the patterns in kilims, which also make the signature of the weaver and the changing conditions of the material visible ("to and fro in shadow from inner to outer shadow"). "For me patterns are really self-contained sound-groupings that enable me to break off without preparation into something else...I use it to see that patterns are 'complete' in themselves, and in no need of development" (durchgeführt) – "only of extension." Extension, enhancement, expansion is a matter of degree, of the scale (Maßstabs) that has nothing to do with a musical 'phrase' or a yardstick. It is something *between* intuition and the planning of patterns ("from impenetrable self to impenetrable unself by way of neither"). "It seems that scale (this subliminal mathematics) is not given to us in Western culture, but must be arrived at individually in our own work and in our own way. Like that Turkish 'tile' rug, it is Rothko's scale that removes any argument over the proportions of one area to another, or over its degree of symmetry or asymmetry. The sum of the parts does not equal the whole; rather, scale is discovered and contained as an image. It is not form that floats the painting, but Rothko's finding that particular scale which suspends all proportions in equilibrium."

The kilims, the music – the in-between with their same, yet not the same patterns in a micro-chromatic colour-scale. One like the other, only now so visible, so audible.

"then no sound
  then gently light unfading on that unheeded neither"

References

A. Bandsma and Robin Brandt. *Flatweaves of Turkey*, London: Philip Wilson Publishers, 2003.

Morton Feldman, "Crippled Symmetry", in: *Res: anthropology and aesthetics*, no. 2, Autumn 1981, pp. 91–103.

Alois Riegl, *Altorienltalische Teppiche* (Leipzig 1892), Nachdruck Mittenwald: Mäander, 1979.

Arwed Tomm, *Streifenkelims*, Aachen: Tomm 2005.

Hans Wilfling, *Teppich-Motive der Turkvölker*, Wien: Braumüller, 1985.

English quotations are taken, unless otherwise noted, from the short text by Samuel Beckett *Neither*, on which Feldman's opera of the same name is based.